Perfect Phrases for Performance Reviews

Perfect Phrases for Performance Reviews

Hundreds of Ready-to-Use Phrases That Describe Your Employees' Performance (from "Unacceptable" to "Outstanding")

Douglas Max
Robert Bacal

McGraw-Hill

New York Chicago San Francisco Lisbon
London Madrid Mexico City Milan New Delhi
San Juan Seoul Singapore Sydney Toronto

Copyright © 2003 by The McGraw-Hill Companies, Inc. Printed in the United States of America. Except as permitted under the United States Copyright Act of 1976, no part of this publication may be reproduced or distributed in any form or by any means, or stored in a data base or retrieval system, without the prior written permission of the publisher.

17 18 19 20 21 22 DOC/DOC 0 9 8 7

ISBN 0-07-140838-X

This is a *CWL Publishing Enterprises Book* produced for McGraw-Hill by CWL Publishing Enterprises, Madison, WI, www.cwlpub.com.

This publication is designed to provide accurate and authoritative information in regard to the subject matter covered. It is sold with the understanding that neither the author nor the publisher is engaged in rendering legal, accounting, or other professional services. If legal advice or other expert assistance is required, the services of a competent professional person should be sought.
> —*From a Declaration of Principles jointly adopted by a Committee of the American Bar Association and a Committee of Publishers*

McGraw-Hill books are available at special quantity discounts to use as premiums and sales promotions, or for use in corporate training programs. For more information, please write to the Director of Special Sales, Professional Publishing, McGraw-Hill, Two Penn Plaza, New York, NY 10121-2298. Or contact your local bookstore.

Contents

Contents

Part Three. Perfect Phrases for Performance Appraisal

Contents

Contents

Topics by Job Category

General Job Skills/Traits

Contents

Contents

Contents

Appendix A.
Ten Mistakes Managers
Make When Conducting
Performance Appraisals   **169**

Appendix B.
Seven Mistakes Employees
Make During Performance Appraisals   **173**

Preface

Performance reviews are a delicate matter. Most managers want to write good, fair, and professional performance appraisals, but it's not always easy to find the "perfect phrase."

This book makes it easy by providing hundreds of "perfect phrases" managers can use on performance appraisal forms, to describe the performance of any employee in 74 skill areas-from "Accuracy" to "Initiative" to "Productivity" to "Time Management Skills." Managers can choose phrases from five performance levels that are used on many performance appraisal forms:

1. Outstanding
2. Exceeds Expectations
3. Meets Expectations
4. Needs Improvement
5. Unacceptable

The phrases include general descriptions of employee performance, such as "shows strong initiative," as well as specific behavioral recommendations, such as "needs repeated instruction when learning a new task."

Part One of this book includes some general tips on planning and conducting a performance appraisal. Part Two shows some examples of performance appraisal forms, using the phrases in this book. Part Three, the core of the book, contains hundreds of "perfect phrases" to describe performance and provide direction for improvement on a performance appraisal form.

Using this book will make it easier to appraise direct reports quickly and fairly. It will give you the phrases you need to accurately describe their performance and help you help them improve their skills and guide their career development.

Acknowledgments

This book is the result of a collaboration. John Woods of CWL Publishing Enterprises asked us to take this project on. We agreed, seeing the value of this for anyone who administers performance appraisals. Richard Narramore of McGraw-Hill, who initiated the project, has been helpful and supportive throughout its development. Bob Magnan and Nancy Woods, also of CWL, edited the manuscript and have a lot to do with the final product you now hold. We thank them all.

Douglas Max
Robert Bacal

Part One

Background for Conducting Performance Reviews

How to Plan, Conduct, and Write a Performance Review

Undertaking formal performance appraisals is not usually an activity most managers relish, but it's an important part of the job of a manager. And it gives you an opportunity, when done correctly, to positively affect the future of your employees. Conducting an effective appraisal means more than just filling out the form your company uses, however. What goes on before you fill out the form is critical to getting the results you're looking for.

However, if you want to simply fill out the form, skip ahead to Part Two. But if you need some help in thinking about and preparing for the appraisals you have to conduct, continue reading.

As part of the appraisal process in many organizations, the manager and employee have a meeting where the manager explains the appraisal process and the criteria for judging performance. If the process involves goals, the manager and employee discuss and agree on what both of them would like to see achieved over a certain time period (usually a year) and, perhaps, the kind of resources the employee will need to succeed. If you are responsible for defining employee goals, then use the initial meeting to explain these goals (and how you will work together to achieve those goals, if appropriate).

Throughout the year, document significant behaviors that are worthy of discussing during a performance review. Just keep notes as you observe the performance of your employees. It's simple and easy to do—far easier than waiting until the end of the year and then trying to recollect what happened.

Setting Performance Goals

What is a goal? It's an agreed-upon statement of what an employee will achieve in a specified period of time. A goals statement should also explain the resources necessary to achieve the goals and how you and your employee will measure success.

Each goal should be measurable, attainable, moderately difficult, and accepted by the employee. Here are some examples:

- Number of rejected items from manufacturing line will not exceed .3% per week.
- Sales per quarter will increase by 5%.
- Expense account will not exceed budget.
- Sign up 5 new customers per month.

In other words, goals should be measurable and aimed at improving the performance of the employee.

Why do we write goals? Written goals allow you to both measure and recognize achievement. They also let you identify and correct performance problems, and they enable you to identify and focus on your top priorities. Aim to limit the number of long-term goals to no more than five. You can also write additional short-term goals for projects that can be completed in a few weeks or months.

How to Plan, Conduct, and Write a Performance Review

How do you write goals? To write goals, you'll first need to collect information from your own records and those of your employees. The next section will explain the kind of information you might use.

What kind of information will you need? This question is best answered by you and your employees, because it depends on the specific situation and each job. Some guidelines:

Most goals will relate to productivity that is generally expressed in terms that include

- Volume of work
- Accuracy of work
- Time to produce X
- Cost per unit of X

Volume measures the amount of work performed, for example, the number of

- orders entered
- cartons packed
- requisitions written
- documents filed

Accuracy measures the degree to which the work is performed free of error, or the quality of the work, for example, the percentage of

- orders entered accurately vs. inaccurately
- cartons packed correctly vs. incorrectly
- requisitions written correctly vs. incorrectly
- documents filed accurately vs. inaccurately

Time measures the duration of the work performed, per hour, per day, per week, per month, per year. Examples include

- claims processed per hour/day/week
- requisitions received and written on the 1st day/2nd day/3rd day
- documents received and filed on the 1st day/2nd day/3rd day

Cost measures the dollars spent for work performed, for example,

$$\frac{\text{Average number of orders per day by the department}}{\text{Average daily wage for department}} = y$$

$$\frac{\text{Average number of claims processed per day by employee}}{\text{Average hourly wage for department}} = y$$

$$\text{Number of requisition errors resulting in rewrites} * \text{Cost per rewrite} = y$$

What if goal achievement is difficult to measure? There may be times when an employee has goals that you *cannot* easily measure. This does not mean that you should not have such goals. Just be certain to have some criteria for evaluating the level of achievement. Here are some examples:

- **Monthly reports.** "Performance is acceptable when I turn in completed monthly reports no more than two times late in any four-month period, without more than one incident of it being more than one week late in any six-month period, and when it is accepted by my boss in all cases with no more than two revisions that are completed in no more than one week."
- **Forecasting.** "I will not fail to bring to my boss's attention adverse trends in my performance before the failure point is

reached, no more than two times in any 12-month period."
- **Employee development.** "Performance is acceptable when training, motivation, and appraisal are discussed during at least two meetings annually between me and each of my direct reports."

Documenting Critical Incidents and Significant Behaviors

An important part of the appraisal process involves recording incidents and behaviors that are out of the ordinary. These are referred to as "critical incidents" and "significant behaviors." A critical incident is behavior that is usually extreme (either good or bad) and that should be recorded for legal reasons, for disciplinary measures, or for purposes of recognizing exemplary actions "above and beyond the call of duty." A significant behavior is one that can make a real difference in an employee's performance.

There are many reasons you should keep record of employees' significant behaviors:

- It increases the accuracy of the performance appraisal, because it's based on documentation rather than memory.
- It provides evidence to support ratings.
- It helps guarantee that you'll consider the performance during the entire appraisal period.
- It reduces bias that occurs when you rate only the most recent behavior.

To be as accurate as possible, write significant behaviors down *as soon as possible* after you have observed the behavior. Record only the specific behavioral facts of the case. Do not include opinions. Do not rely on hearsay! To ensure that the documentation is a representative record of an individual's performance, document performance during the entire appraisal period.

In documenting behaviors, be consistent in how you do it. Use the same format and the same level of detail with each individual. Document both productive and unproductive behaviors. Documenting significant behaviors helps to make the performance evaluation interview more productive. You'll be more confident going into the interview if you have a record of behaviors to back up your ratings because you'll be more confident you're rating your employee accurately.

Documenting significant behavior helps improve communication in the interview. There is less likelihood to be disagreement about whether an event occurred or not when you have documented behaviors and incidents. It helps keep the tone of the entire appraisal constructive rather than judgmental. Instead of dealing with impressions, you're dealing with *specific examples* of performance. The discussion can focus on how the performance can be improved in the future. Employees are better able to see their deficiencies. They know what they must do in order to improve.

The feedback to employees, both positive and critical, from significant behaviors can enhance employee motivation to improve. When an employee sees that specific behaviors are noted and appreciated, he or she will feel good and work harder to generate such feedback. In the case of behaviors that undermine performance, the employee may not have been aware of the problems. Here are some examples of significant behaviors you might note:

- Customer called after hours with urgent need for a replacement part to deal with an emergency situation. Employee

personally delivered part, substantially reinforcing the loyalty of an important customer.
- Made specific suggestion on manufacturing process that resulted in $50,000 in savings over a six-month period.
- Angrily reacted to an incident on the shop floor that intimidated other employees and made it more difficult to investigate what happened.

Accurate documentation of specific behavior and incidents allows an employee to understand which on-the-job behaviors are productive and which are not. Such information gives employees what they need to improve.

Writing the Appraisal

If you've collected significant behaviors during this appraisal period, then the first step in writing an appraisal that will result in improved or continued good performance is to review these notes. Review also any results or other metrics you have to judge how well the employee has met his or her goals.

Even if your appraisal form only calls for you to "check a box," you generally can add additional comments to justify or explain the rating. In fact, if the appraisal process is to have any value to the employee, you must provide more information than a numeric rating. If you aren't required to make comments, you may want to consider including them on the appraisal form anyway.

Combined with the significant behavior statements and actual work results, you're most of the way to completing a form and documenting an effective appraisal.

Common Performance Review Errors

Another thing you'll want to do is to review the common errors made during the appraisal process. It's a wee bit more complicated than you think—the business of providing fair and objective feedback to employees—because … well, you're human. You can easily avoid or reduce errors by understanding what errors are common and following the suggestions below for dealing with them.

Contrast Error. The tendency to evaluate a person relative to other individuals, rather than on the requirements of the job. An example would be rating someone low, even though he or she was above average, because everyone else in the department is superior. A review should be based on comparing performance with established criteria.

First-Impression Error. The tendency to make an initial favorable or unfavorable judgment, which judgment serves as the basis for appraising future performance. All subsequent information is ignored or perceptually distorted. By considering behavior throughout the rating period, you'll reduce this error.

Recency Effect. The tendency to give extra weight to what you have seen recently and diminish the importance of observations you may have made earlier in the review period. In some cases it may be appropriate to weight recent behavior more than old behavior, particularly if it shows improvement. Otherwise, be sure to consider the entire period of appraisal.

Halo Effect. Generalizing from one aspect of performance to all aspects of performance. People have strengths and weaknesses. It is important to evaluate all aspects of performance throughout the period of the review.

Devil Effect. The opposite of the halo effect, generalizing from one or two negative aspects of performance and become blind to the positive aspects of the performance.

Similar-to-Me Effect. The tendency to judge more favorably those people whose background is similar to yours. The more similar the attitudes and background, the greater the tendency to judge that individual favorably. Appraise performance and behaviors, not personality or background.

Central Tendency. Occurs when an employee is consistently rated at or near the midpoint of the scale, regardless of the actual level of performance. This is a problem for several reasons. Such evaluations don't differentiate between good and bad performers. And they're particularly damaging to the motivation of high achievers, and they don't provide a realistic basis for discussing actual performance and improvements during the appraisal discussion.

Negative or Positive Leniency. Occurs when an employee is rated too hard (negative leniency) or too easy (positive leniency). Again, it creates a problem because the appraisal doesn't reflect true performance. With negative leniency, good performers may get tired of trying to perform well; no matter what they do, they'll be rated lower. With positive leniency, employees may have unrealistic expectations about raises, promotions, or other career gains.

To reduce rating errors:

- Ensure that the criteria being used are job related.
- Rate employees in relation to the job responsibilities.
- Put other people's input into proper perspective and don't weigh it too heavily. If you feel that this additional input warrants any changes in the appraisal, discuss it with your boss.

■ Consider all performance dimensions and realize that they are not always related. A person can do very well on one dimension and perform poorly on another.

■ Don't rate people in any particular order. Do not rate all the best or worst performers first.

■ Do not compare the ratings of employees until after all employee evaluations are complete.

Legal Issues

When an employment situation becomes a legal situation, there's no substitute for proof—you must have records or other evidence proving that an employee did or did not do something ... whether it's stealing, lying, or being late too many times.

What may be more important is that you document the communication you have with employees, particularly when it involves discussion of performance problems. Generally, if you have not notified or discussed problems with the employee and documented those discussions, you have less backup if the employee accuses you of discrimination or similar charges. That means ensuring that the employee signs any documents you keep about communication with the employee.

Be on the alert for performance that's out of the ordinary, either good or bad, and make a note of it. That way, when it comes time to do the appraisal review, you'll be prepared, and you'll be similarly prepared for court, should it ever come to that.

The best way to deal with legal issues is to prevent them by conducting a competent, fair appraisal; demonstrating that you've invested a lot of time analyzing this employee's performance. Then conduct the review as we suggest and you'll substantially minimize the chances that your conduct would lead to a suit or other legal action. Here are some specifics to remember:

- Keep copies of HR records even if the HR department also has these records.
- Maintain accurate performance data.
- Meet regularly with employees to provide the feedback and information they need to perform well, also reducing any surprises and the motivation to sue.
- Document, document, document.

Conducting the Review

How to talk about your employees' performance. The first thing you can do to conduct an effective performance appraisal is to make sure that there are no surprises in store for the employee. This means that you should have communicated with your employees on a regular basis about how they are doing with their particular assignments and how they are collaborating with others.

The formal appraisal session should be mainly a way to summarize and continue the informal interaction that has previously taken place between you and your employees. It should also be a time to look at how you and the employee can continue to work well together in the future. Your job in this session is not to tell the employee all the things you think he or she did wrong over the past year. One reason performance appraisal sessions are often dreaded is that managers and employees feel the managers have to find something to criticize about the person being appraised. What can happen in that situation is that the manager might mention a negative comment the employee made or the fact that the employee was late to work two times over the past six months or similar trivial points. This causes the employee to feel resentful and become defensive.

Approach the person you're appraising as a partner rather than a judge. This will minimize hostility. Also, by focusing on your employee's development rather than on fault-finding, you'll set a positive tone and the discussion will become more productive and easier for both of you.

You may be conducting a performance review because it's required, but it's also a great opportunity to help your employees achieve job goals. Talk with your employees one on one about your expectations for them. Talk about goals, resources to help them achieve these goals, and what you're planning on doing to help. With some, you'll set goals to meet certain performance results; with others, you might set target levels for different "ratings"; for others, the goals might be relating to on-the-job behavior; for others still, the goals might target both behaviors and results.

Set goals, work toward them with your employees, and discuss what happened at the next review—easier said than done! Nevertheless, employees want to know where they stand. They want to receive feedback on their performance. Both ongoing discussions and periodic performance appraisals enable you to provide employees with this information.

Tell them the purpose. Since performance helps determine salary, job assignments, transfers, promotions, demotions, and termination, it is important to tell the employee that you're rating his or her performance based on responsibilities and goals.

The appraisal discussion is also a time to discuss the employee's job expectations and the organization's expectation of the employee. You should also encourage the employee to talk about any other job-related issues or concerns.

How to Plan, Conduct, and Write a Performance Review

Minimize reluctance. Many employees are not enthusiastic about performance appraisals because previous ones seemed "a waste of time" or unpleasant. Your skill will determine whether employees regard the discussion with enthusiasm or dread. You can change their attitudes by listening to their concerns and by explaining how you plan to handle the meeting and that the main purpose to help you both improve.

Gain the employee's commitment. You want the employee to actively participate in the entire appraisal process. This can happen if the employee understands that it will be a two-way discussion of performance. The employee should also understand that the purpose of the appraisal is to recognize success and plan improvement where necessary.

To ensure your appraisal meeting is successful, review the recommendations below and then follow the steps outlined later to help guide you through the meeting.

- Discuss actual performance data/significant behaviors.
- Compare data with responsibilities/goals.
- Rate performance (if appropriate in your appraisal system).
- Maintain positive focus.
- Focus on solving problems, not finding fault.
- Solicit and use input from employees.
- Evaluate objectively.
- Provide recognition.
- Discuss specific actions for you and the employee to take.
- Express confidence.

Discuss actual performance data/significant behaviors. If the performance appraisal discussion is to be effective, you should have performance data and significant behaviors for each area of measurement. The employee should have access to this same data before the appraisal session. Both you and the employee must feel that the data is objective and accurate. If the employee reviews the data prior to the appraisal, you can handle any question about its objectivity and accuracy before the appraisal discussion.

Compare data with responsibilities/goals. This way both you and the employee know whether he or she has met, exceeded, or missed the goals for the job. Before the session in some organizations, it is the employee's responsibility to also prepare data on goal achievement.

Rate performance. Rate the employee's performance in each area of measurement, based upon actual data. The ratings should take into account any factors outside the employee's control that contributed to achieving or failing to achieve his or her goals. It's a good idea to discuss your ratings with your immediate supervisor so that both of you are confident that your ratings are justifiable.

Maintain positive focus. If the employee's overall performance rating is satisfactory, the emphasis of feedback should be that he or she is doing well. Allow sufficient time to discuss and recognize those areas where performance met or exceeded goals. Exploring the factors that led to success will help you and the employee build on strengths to increase productivity in the future.

Focus on solving problems, not finding fault. In those areas where the employee is not meeting expectations with regard to responsibilities or goals, the emphasis should be on identifying the causes, focusing on solutions, and outlining specific actions that will enable the employee to meet those expectations. The discussion should be future-oriented, focusing on plans for improvement. Expression of concern with past poor perform-ance should be balanced with recognition of achievements, if overall performance is satisfactory.

Solicit and use input from employees. You should actively involve the employee in the performance appraisal discussion. In addition to sharing performance data and participating in the problem-solving discussion, the employee may also have addi-tional items or concerns to discuss. Be prepared to discuss these items openly and work toward solutions. The employee may want to discuss salary, career opportunities, or barriers to satis-factory performance, such as insufficient resources, lack of man-agement support, etc. If you cannot adequately address such issues during the appraisal discussion, you should set a follow-up date to discuss these items at length.

Evaluate objectively. This means that you're focusing on per-formance and the factors that led to success or the obstacles that got in the way of success. You are not evaluating the person but his or her performance in a fair and dispassionate way. If the employee knows this is what you are doing and that both of you are there to help each other succeed, the session will be much more productive.

Provide recognition. Praise the employee for those things done well. When you praise, you're helping the person know what he or she is doing well in order to continue to do those things. It also creates a positive tone for the session.

Discuss specific actions for you and the employee to take. At the conclusion of the session, list specific actions the employee will take to finish old business, take on new goals, and improve his or her skills. Also list the actions you will take to support the employee in these activities.

Express confidence. Let the employee know that you feel good about his or her abilities and that you're there to help the employee succeed and that you're confident that, working together, this will happen and that you are glad to be working with him or her.

Making the Session Go Smoothly

As you undertake appraisal, here are some ways you can make the actual session go smoothly:

- Put the employee at ease at the start of the session. Do this by acknowledging that these sessions can be a little nerve-wracking, but that the purpose is to help everyone in the work group improve and to gather information on how to help these improvement efforts.
- Ask the employee what he or she thinks of his or her total performance—not just strong or weak areas. In this way, you get an overall sense of how the employee thinks he or she is doing.
- Question the employee about what he or she thinks his or her personal strengths are. This chance to describe what he or she does best helps the employee feel positive about the appraisal.
- Tell the employee what you believe his or her strengths are. This demonstrates that you are paying attention to performance.
- Describe those areas where you think the employee might improve; use documentation to demonstrate why you are

making these observations. Then ask the employee what he or she thinks of this and listen silently to the response. His or her reasons for poor performance or problems on the job might include lack of training, personality conflicts with other employees, misunderstandings about expectations or responsibilities, lack of knowledge about how to use new equipment, and physical obstacles, such as poor lighting or poorly maintained equipment.

- Assuming that you can identify the cause of poor performance, ask the employee what you two can do together to take care of it.
- Set new goals for performance for the next appraisal period.
- Keep a record of the meeting, including a timetable for performance improvement and what each of you will do to ensure that happens.
- Be open and honest, yet considerate of the employee's feelings. The goal is to facilitate improvement for the individual, the team, and the organization.

After the appraisal session, it's vital to follow up on what you and the employee have agreed on during the session. It indicates that you and the organization are serious about improvement.

- Mark your calendar to meet with individual employees to review their progress.
- Set up training as needed to address skill deficiencies.
- If a personal problem is involved, arrange for the employee to get counseling, if it is available.
- If an employee continues to perform poorly, make him or her aware of the consequences (discipline, demotion, or termination).

■ Provide positive feedback when you see improvements in performance.

How to Talk About Salary

Performance reviews are often held as separate meetings from discussions about salary. If it's this way in your company, then you should explain that to the employee as well as the reasons for doing it this way.

Presumably it's because the focus of the discussion is performance and not money, which will be considered at another time.

You may, though, be able to tell employees more, such as that their performance was superior and that it will bring them nearer the higher bonuses or that their overall performance was below par, and so that's approximately what they might expect with their bonus.

If an employee is adamant about discussing salary and it's against the policy in your company, then you should schedule a meeting to discuss that topic.

Perfect Phrases for Performance Reviews

When documenting performance or justifying the rating you've given an employee, try to focus on behaviors and results. Work on finding a phrase that best describes how you judge the person's performance in a particular area. Helping you do that is the purpose of this book, but you should, of course, modify these phrases to fit your particular situation. Since there are many related categories in the phrases in Part Three, be sure to check all appropriate categories to find phrases that will work best for you in a particular situation.

For example, take a phrase like "exceedingly competent," delete "exceedingly," and you're left with "competent." Substitute "not very," "sometimes," etc. and you've got an entirely different meaning—something that may more accurately reflect the shade of meaning you're looking for.

There are two types of phrases or items in each category. One type describes that characteristic in general terms; the other type includes some more behavioral or results-oriented phrases you might use in the appraisal. For these behavioral items, you should, of course, include your own terms, numbers, etc. and place them under the appropriate rating on the form you're using.

You might also use these concrete items to establish goals or as the basis for creating a rating scale. For example, you'll give an employee an "outstanding" or a "5" rating if she makes 1% or fewer errors, an "exceeds expectations" or "4" for 2%-5% errors, and so on.

Part Two

Examples of Forms for Performance Reviews

Performance Appraisal Review Forms

The purpose of this book is to provide you with hundreds of phrases to facilitate the performance appraisal process. In keeping with that goal, this part of the book includes a few examples of appraisal forms used in three organizations. All of these are different from one another, yet all require the person doing the appraising to include descriptive phrases such as found in Part Three.

We have edited and reformatted these forms to fit in this book. The parts of the forms that would use phrases like those included in this book are filled in. The other parts are included so you can see the entire form, including instructions on one of them that define levels of performance and the parts that require the manager and employee to put down their thoughts and goals for the next review period. You can use these examples for models as you use this book to undertake your appraisals.

Performance Expectations/Review

Key Results Expected:

10% reduction in waste
5 suggestions for improvement from all employees
and so on

Key Job Competencies:

Competency Group	Competency	Examples/Comments
Communication	Facilitate Communication	Effectively builds interactivity with others
	Oral Communication	Articulate and well-organized
	Written Communication	Writes quickly, clearly, and correctly
Continuous Improvement	Initiative and innovation	Is above the norm in showing initiative
	Flexibility	Will reset priorities as required
	Technical Expertise	Has mastered SPC techniques
Leadership	Leadership	Led group to exceed sales targets in 14 of 15 regions
	Empowering Others	Turns on the motivation for excellece among employees
	Use of Influence	Demeanor sets an example for others
	Coaching	Delivers feedback directly and constructively
Teamwork	Professional Conduct	Manages the team process with great skill
	Responsiveness	Keeps others informed of status of projects affecting them

We have discussed and agreed upon the above performance competencies.

_____   _____
Employee Signature   **Manager Signature**

Example 1. A form with the focus on competencies

Performance Planning and Review Document	

Employee's Name:	Postition Title:
Hire Date:	Review Date:
Department:	Supervisor's Name:

Items for Discussion	Supervisor's Comments (Required)
Professionalism	
Attitude	Direct, straightforward, and honest. Always focuses on getting things done.
Acceptance of Responsibility	Williingly accepts responsibility for new projects.
Dependability	Always delivers on promises.
Professional/Personal Growth	Demonstrates continuous learning.
Work	
Job Knowledge	Maintains knowledge through training and seminars.
Work Quality	Quality of outputs meets standards.
Customer Service	Solves customer problems with speed and accuracy.
Communication	Articulate and well-organized speaker.
Teamwork	Mostly an optimistic team player.
Flexibility	Able to shift focus rapidly.
Safe/Unsafe Work Practices	Has violated a safety rule only once.
Optional Factors	
Employee-Input Form	
Attached and discussed	

Example 2. Form that focuses on job characteristics (p. 1)

Performance Planning and Review Document
Additional comments by Supervisor:
Comments by Employee:
Other performance issues discussed during this review period: ____ Yes, please indicate if other documentation exists ... ____ No
Supervisor and employee are required to sign the form. Signatures indicate that supervisor and employee have discussed performance and the comments written on this document. Signatures do not necessarily indicate agreement. **Supervisor's Signature:**   **Date:** **Employee's Signature:**   **Date:** **Next-Level Supervisor's Signature:**   **Date:**

Example 2. A form that focuses on job characteristics (p. 2)

Performance Appraisal	
Employee's Name	**Title:**
Review Period __/__/__ to __/__/__	**Employee SSN**
Work Location	**Supervisor's Name:**
Type of Review ___ 90 day ___Performance	

INSTRUCTIONS

1. Rating: Rate the employee in each job area, unless it is not applicable, by placing the rating in the box that best indicates where the employee stands in relation to the accountability. Every factor must be either rated or marked "NA/NO" (Not applicable/Not observed). Indicate the overall rating at the end of the job areas.

2. Remarks: Use the "Remarks" space after each job area to explain in more detail or to give examples of that area. All except level 3 require comments .

3. Summary: Complete the Major Accomplishments, Job-Related Strengths, Areas for Improvement/Development, Action Plan sections. Have the employee complete the Employee Comments section. Use additional sheets if needed.

4. Human Resources Review: Human Resources must review and sign the evaluation before the actual review is conducted.

5. Signatures: Sign the review and have the employee sign before submitting the original form to Human Resources for filing in the employee's personnel file.

Ratings and Meanings:

5 Performance consistently exceeds job requirements. Demonstrates unusually high level of performance relative to all assignments and objectives. Distinguished performance overall.

4 Performance meets and often exceeds job requirements. Demonstrates successful performance on all major assignments and objectives and consistently exceeds position requirements in some areas.

3 Performance consistently meets job requirements. Demonstrates successful performance on all or most major assignments and objectives.

2 Performance is inconsistent; meets some job requirements but not consistently. Overall performance is below the acceptable level and must improve to meet minimum position requirements.

1 Performance is consistently below job requirements. Fails to meet position requirements in most areas. A corrective action plan and performance improvement are mandatory.

NA/NO This accountability is not applicable or has not been observed by the reviewer.

Example 3. A form that uses numerical ratings (p. 1)

Job Area	Remarks	Rating
1. *Professional Knowledge/Work Knowledge/Skills:* Possesses and applies knowledge or skills necessary for task completion. Keeps current on new developments in area of work.	Knowledge exceeds what is required to perform well.	4
2. *Quality of Work:* Assignments are accurate, complete, and comply with objectives.	Performs efficiently and well.	3
3. *Quantity of Work:* Produces significant volume of work to support goals within specified time frames.	Work is regularly completed on time and error free.	3
4. *Communication:* Maintains open, effective communications with all employees and clients. Written and verbal communications are clear, concise, and understandable.	Can explain complicated procedures well. Can express herself clearly in written communication.	4
5. *Teamwork:* Willingly cooperates, shares information, assists, and is tolerant of others in daily interaction with all employees, vendors, and clients.	Gets along well with fellow team members.	3
6. *Reliability:* Can be relied upon to complete tasks and follow up as needed.	Does not disappoint when deadlines are tight.	4
7. *Adaptability/Flexibility:* Easily adjusts to changes in routine, assignments, and company/client needs and continues to be productive.	Willingly assumes others' tasks in case of absences.	5
8. *Initiative:* Voluntarily recommends resourceful, alternative, or original ideas/procedures for work improvement or problem solution.	Will take risks to accommodate customers. Instituted extranet connection for vendor X to improve project coordination.	4
9. *Planning/Scheduling:* Prioritizes tasks, anticipates needs, and makes adjustments.	Others regularly rely on her scheduling abilities.	5
10. *Problem Solving:* Identifies problems within own area, develops resourceful solutions, and makes recommendations for corrective action.	Thorough in analyzing and developing solutions.	4

Example 3. Part of page 2 of the same form, laying out specific characteristics, with definitions of each area, places for comments and a space for numerical ratings

Summary
Sections 1, 2, 3, and 4 should be completed by the supervisor. Section 5 should be completed by the employee.
1. Major accomplishments since last review
2. Job-related strengths
3. Areas for improvement/development
4. Action plan
5. Employee comments

Signatures
I acknowledge that this review has been discussed with me. My signature does not imply agreement or disagreement.

Employee: Date:

  Supervisor: Date:

  Human Resources: Date:

Example 3. A form that shows numerical ratings (p. 3)

Part Three

Perfect Phrases for Performance Reviews

Contents (Alphabetical)

Contents (by Topic)

General Job Skills/Traits

Technical Skills

Productivity

Management/Leadership/Supervisory

Management Control

Communications/Interpersonal

Personal Qualities/Characteristics

Accuracy

Outstanding
- Maintains high accuracy under tight deadlines
- Mistakes don't slip through
- Achieves zero errors when required
- Trusted to do tasks demanding high accuracy
- Less than 1% error rate

Exceeds Expectations
- Takes pride in accuracy and makes effort to improve
- Maintains accuracy even under pressure
- Managers have commented on high level of accuracy
- Identifies own errors early on

Meets Expectations
- Checks finished product before forwarding
- Uses technical tools to improve accuracy (e.g., spellchecker)
- Does not require constant supervision
- Balances accuracy with speed

Needs Improvement
- Sometimes makes small errors
- Less than 5% errors but more than 2%
- Excessively concerned about being perfect
- Does not check work before submitting
- Tends to miss small mistakes

Unacceptable
- Errors have caused money loss
- Mistakes have caused customer loss
- Error rate over ___%
- ___ customers have complained about errors
- Misses small and large mistakes

Administrative Skills

Outstanding
- Has improved many departmental procedures
- Effectively tracks the status of projects
- Handles many tasks simultaneously
- Documents are always ready when needed
- Created important new record-keeping systems
- Uses advanced PowerPoint functions

Exceeds Expectations
- Streamlined many procedures
- Administers accounts payable and receivable without error
- Administers many functions without error
- Thorough, reliable, and accurate
- Maintains vital information
- Sets priorities well

Meets Expectations
- Files and finds documents with ease
- Has all the administrative skills required
- Maintains important records
- Writes clear memos
- Sets priorities to ensure documents are ready when needed
- Uses software effectively
- Knows enough PowerPoint to create effective presentations

Needs Improvement
- Loses essential data occasionally
- Some records can't be found or are inaccurate
- Sometimes does not maintain records

➡

- Reports are lost on occasion
- Administration is a weakness
- Cannot create graphs
- Rarely relies on the computer to simplify tasks
- Makes grammatical and punctuation errors in memos

Unacceptable
- Administrative skills are negligible
- Memos are often unclear
- Uses condescending tone in staff memos
- Formatting errors make documents unusable
- Reports are often misfiled and lost
- Has missed a number of important deadlines

Analytic Skills

Outstanding

- Has outstanding analytic skills
- Can zero in on the cause of a problem and develop solutions
- Can perceive relationships in a mass of data
- Excellent analyst
- Translates analysis into actions that fit
- Communicates analysis results clearly and concisely

Exceeds Expectations

- Possesses good analytic skills
- Analysis shows insight
- Methodical analyst
- In six production failures, made a diagnosis and repair within two hours
- Communicates analysis results clearly to others

Meets Expectations

- Detail oriented
- Possesses the skills to solve basic on-the-job problems
- Analyzes data and makes appropriate recommendations
- Summarizes reports from five supervisors in time for Monday managers' meetings

Needs Improvement

- Needs to develop skills to analyze situations
- Frequently draws wrong conclusions from data
- Doesn't do detailed analysis
- Analysis sometimes focuses on the unimportant
- Delegates research

- Analytic results are questioned by others
- Makes analytic errors regularly
- Makes mathematical errors
- Errors caused problems in 3 out of 10 instances

Unacceptable
- Analysis is limited
- Does not have the analytic skills required
- Analytic skills are below what's necessary
- Frequently comes to the wrong conclusions
- Was unable to solve problems for 7 out of 10 customers on helpline

Appraisal and Evaluation Skills

Outstanding
- Conscientiously gathers information to fairly appraise
- Exceptionally fair
- Involves staff in appraisals
- Uses appraisal to build commitment and motivation
- Provides substantial documentation of performance
- Conducts appraisals on time
- Bases appraisal on pre-agreed goals
- Negotiates fair and appropriate goals
- Negotiates stretch goals to help employees improve

Exceeds Expectations
- Puts employees at ease
- Gains employees' motivation to perform better in the future
- Gets staff involved in the appraisal process
- Evaluations free from bias
- Performance focused
- Creates positive, developmental-focused tone
- Explains appraisal process clearly
- Prepares documents prior to each appraisal
- Negotiates goals

Meets Expectations
- Unbiased
- Handles appraisal responsibilities well
- Believes in the importance of appraisal
- Appraises job performance fairly
- Uses appraisals to achieve departmental goals
- Develops employees with appraisal process
- Involves employees in setting goals

- Records employees' reactions
- Documents significant behaviors

Needs Improvement
- Uncomfortable with appraisals
- Doesn't listen
- Rarely gets staff involved
- Critical, not developmental
- Gives goals, doesn't negotiate
- Appraisal discussions are one-sided
- Employees regularly disagree with appraisals

Unacceptable
- Biased ratings
- Does not set goals at beginning of appraisal period
- Appraisal documents are frequently late
- Does not involve staff in appraisal process
- Dictates, never negotiates goals with staff members
- Makes many rater errors
- Spends only __ minutes on appraisal

Attendance

Outstanding
- Always at work and on time
- Great attendance record
- Makes it to work unless seriously ill
- Never misses work without prior and appropriate notification
- Arrives at work at least __ minutes early every day
- Has missed only one day due to sickness in last three years

Exceeds Expectations
- Consistently arrives at work early
- Good attendance
- Has rarely missed work due to illness
- Clocks in at least five minutes early every day
- Has missed only two days because of illness

Meets Expectations
- Consistently arrives at work on time
- Attendance satisfactory
- Only misses work due to verified illness
- Leaves home early on inclement days to arrive on time
- Has not used more than allotted sick days
- Back from lunch on time

Needs Improvement
- Takes longer breaks than appropriate
- Arrives late at least one day a month
- Has missed work without prior notification 10 times this year
- Consistently uses all sick days
- Has arrived __ times late by __ minutes or more

Unacceptable

- Poor attendance
- Not dependable
- Breaks are long and too frequent
- Gets to work late at least once a week
- Has used ___ sick days on Fridays or Mondays
- Has used ___ days over allotted sick days
- Does not come to work when it's raining
- Often is late more than ___ minutes
- Has failed to call in sick ___ times

Attitude or Approach to Work

Outstanding
- Cordial and happy to help
- Looks for ways to help others
- Comes to work 15 minutes early each day
- Always upbeat and optimistic
- Views success in relation to group's success
- Enthusiastic and energetic

Exceeds Expectations
- Positive, contagious spirit
- Direct, straightforward, and honest
- Winning attitude
- Always pleasant to be around
- Team player

Meets Expectations
- Rarely down
- Friendly and outgoing
- Cooperative and cordial
- Always focuses on getting things done
- Volunteered to be a member of the WorkLife Committee
- Has "can do" attitude

Needs Improvement
- Can be quarrelsome
- Can be negative
- Projects "in it for myself" attitude
- Rarely helps others
- Needs to be prompted to stop daydreaming
- Creates tension

➡

Unacceptable

- Aloof
- Can be snobbish
- Projects attitude of superiority that turns off other employees
- Presence often creates tension in group
- Not cooperative
- Frequently criticizes others
- Pessimistic
- Always finding fault with others

Coaching

Outstanding
- Coaches many to excel
- A role model, teacher, and guide
- Identifies weaknesses and solutions
- Inspires others to do better
- Outstanding ability to explain and teach

Exceeds Expectations
- Builds independence
- Very supportive of others' attempts at improvement
- Excellent at demonstrating appropriate procedures
- Delivers feedback directly and constructively
- Applauds effort

Meets Expectations
- Times coaching interventions effectively
- Does not overwhelm other person
- Draws out knowledge and skills from others
- Leads people to discover their own answers
- Available when needed
- Allocates time for the coaching process

Needs Improvement
- Isn't effective with people slow to learn
- Guides and coaches, but doesn't let others have responsibility
- Gets frustrated when others aren't learning
- Assumes too much knowledge on others' part
- Doesn't enable staff to reduce dependency
- Has difficulty integrating coaching with rest of job ➡

Unacceptable

- Dictates to others rather than involving them
- Has failed to develop a successor
- Insensitive to needs of other person
- Has reduced other person to tears
- Staff uncomfortable being coached by him/her
- Believes coaching not part of job

Communication Skills, Verbal

Outstanding
- Superior skills on phone and in meetings
- Speaks persuasively and convincingly
- Thoughtful and responsive to employees at all levels
- Is an articulate spokesperson for the team's views
- Builds interactivity with audience
- Develops clear, concise computer presenations

Exceeds Expectations
- Is convincing and confident when speaking
- Prepares for all communications
- Speaks articulately and concisely
- Adept at technical explanations
- Concludes on an upbeat note
- Answers questions directly

Meets Expectations
- Uses collateral material effectively
- Can explain complicated procedures well
- Rarely fumbles for an answer
- Seems comfortable while presenting
- Articulate and well-organized speaker
- Clear, understandable voice

Needs Improvement
- Speaks in monotone
- Is not confident when presenting
- Reads script and has little contact with audience
- Uncomfortable responding to questions
- Makes grammatical mistakes when speaking
- Positions often not clearly thought out

Unacceptable

- Often makes grammatical errors when speaking
- Does not build rapport when speaking with others
- Does not build audience participation when needed
- Often misunderstands what others are saying, leading to mistakes on the job
- Does not know how to ask questions that will guide work

Communication Skills, Written

Outstanding
- Exceptional communicator
- All writing is free of punctuation or grammatical errors
- Clear, concise, error-free writing
- Excellent at persuasive writing
- Wrote bids that gained business 7 out of 10 times
- Regularly receives positive feedback on clarity of writing

Exceeds Expectations
- Written communications easily understood
- Writes quickly, clearly, and correctly
- Uses resources when unsure of proper spelling, punctuation, or grammar
- Uses formatting effectively to highlight key information
- Documentation is consistently understood
- Translations of documentation were free of confusion
- E-mails and memos are clear and to the point

Meets Expectations
- Can express him/herself clearly in written communication
- Competent writer
- Makes few grammar or punctuation errors
- Spelling usually correct
- Conveys information reasonably clearly
- Writes professional communications, including e-mail

Needs Improvement
- The point of a written communication not always clear
- Hard to understand focus in written communications
- Makes grammatical and punctuation errors
- Takes a long time to get to the point

➡

- Written communications sometimes lead to misunderstandings
- Many people were confused about report X

Unacceptable
- Poor writer
- Numerous errors and lack of organization make understanding difficult
- Writing fails to meet company standards
- Writing represents our company poorly
- Many customers failed to understand the August Bulletin
- Poor written communication resulted in errors costing $_____

Computer Skills

Outstanding
- Expert in the use of Excel
- Easily uses the more difficult features of Word
- Solves all software and hardware problems quickly
- Has championed movement to paperless operations
- Designed, implemented, and manages department's intranet site
- Creates forms that are virtually foolproof
- Produced __ documents with only __ requiring rework
- Conducted __ Internet searches, with only __ requiring additional information

Exceeds Expectations
- Shows great skills in all areas
- Strengths are in many of our regularly used programs
- Helps others with advanced computer functions
- Established many protocols for file keeping
- Can quickly learn new programs
- Finds customer records quickly while on the phone
- Formatted __-page document within __ days from receipt of submissions
- Created database with __ fields (__ relational) in __ days
- Redesigned enterprise system to speed processing without affecting users

Meets Expectations
- Competent with all software used
- Can fix minor hardware problems
- Communicates expectations to IT personnel effectively
- Understands Windows basics

➡

- Handles computer problems without getting frustrated
- With the exception of Program X, keeps up with colleagues
- Entered __ customer delivery requests with __ errors

Needs Improvement
- Has difficulty with essential programs
- Makes repeated formatting errors
- Learning new software is a challenge
- Sometimes forgets to turn computer off
- Can't find saved files
- Loaded personal software against policy
- Caused two major system failures

Unacceptable
- Lacks the computer skills this job requires
- Makes repeated errors after repeated instructions
- Has not learned basics
- After six months still has problems finding customer records
- Asks questions found in help file
- Calls helpdesk frequently
- Doesn't heed warning messages
- Deleted required software in error

Conflict Management

Outstanding
- Has resolved several difficult conflicts this year
- Avoids escalation
- Received customer compliments for resolving a conflict
- Made partners out of enemies
- Acted as conflict troubleshooter within organization

Exceeds Expectations
- Looks for common ground
- Listens carefully to both sides
- Builds customer loyalty through conflict management
- Diplomatic without sidestepping critical issues
- Peers seek his/her advice in dealing with conflict situations
- Understands when compromise is needed

Meets Expectations
- Uses basic mediation techniques
- Uses outside personnel when necessary
- Handles conflict in calm, unemotional ways
- Remains calm in tough situations
- Effective third party in handling disputes

Needs Improvement
- Sometimes impatient with disagreement
- Becomes defensive in some conflicts
- Has an ongoing conflict with another staff member
- Starts unnecessary conflict when stressed
- Superiors sometimes need to step in

Unacceptable
- Has made several conflicts worse

- Will not yield in conflict
- Makes compromises rarely
- Argues for trivial reasons
- Often focuses on blaming others
- Does not recognize when outside help needed
- Stubborn
- Attitude can cause conflict

Cooperation

Outstanding
- Does everything asked without objection
- Immediately puts clients' requests above other work
- Works in concert with others
- Unrivaled willingness to help
- Real team player
- Establishes rapport with everyone
- Works on four project teams, while a volunteer on two other teams

Exceeds Expectations
- Always asks others for extra work
- Shares ideas freely
- Will do what it takes to work with others
- Effective representative of department
- Works toward team goals without consideration of personal effect
- Formed team with representatives from departments affected by software program X

Meets Expectations
- Works well with other departments
- Puts good of company above that of department
- Is flexible with priorities
- Willing to cooperate
- Compliant to others' needs
- Received compliments on spirit of cooperation on the XYZ project

Needs Improvement
- Will object to work when it interferes with schedule
- Is often reluctant to help others on the job ➡

- Won't bend on views without coercion
- Shows lack of cooperation on team projects
- Declined an offer to be part of XYZ team

Unacceptable
- Unwilling to cooperate
- Will not change views
- Inflexible and noncompliant
- Refused to follow rules during a spill cleanup
- Consistently neglects to mark hazardous waste according to regulations

Cost Cutting

Outstanding
- Overachieved cost-cutting targets this year
- Invented innovative cost-cutting measures
- Improved profit margin by ___% last year
- Developed company-wide cost-cutting suggestion program

Exceeds Expectations
- Developed methods to identify cost overruns
- Asks for cost-cutting suggestions from staff
- Used techniques (e.g., outsourcing) effectively
- Welcomes and evaluates any cost-cutting ideas

Meets Expectations
- Implemented corporate strategies
- Met cost-cutting goals
- Stays within budgeted guidelines
- Maintained productivity along with modest cost savings
- Treats company money as his/her own

Needs Improvement
- Sacrificed productivity by cutting too deep
- Insists on spending budget even if not needed
- Needs to improve methods for priority spending
- Has taken advantage of perks on travel status

Unacceptable
- Cost-cutting measures backfired
- Unit unable to function properly
- Spends with no reflection
- Supervisors need to scrutinize every expenditure
- Pads expenses

Creativity

Outstanding
- Is one of our most creative designers
- Exceedingly creative
- Changed campaign based on market surveys
- Solved a long-standing software glitch through a creative workaround
- Developed promotional concepts that won five clients
- Contributed workplace improvement ideas that saved the department $__
- Improved name recognition by __% in __ weeks
- Changed a software program to cut processing time by __%

Exceeds Expectations
- Sees things from a unique angle
- Unique perspectives
- Imaginative ideas for difficult problems
- Unique ideas for recurring issues
- Has solved many problems by looking from unique perspective
- Often has the edge our clients want
- Organized motivational field trip for staff
- Comes up with creative ideas often
- Redesigned workflow between departments that cut approval time 10%

Meets Expectations
- Has an appropriate level of creativity
- Imaginative vision
- Developed a number of new ideas for old problems
- Adds a creative flair to projects

➡

- Always experimenting with new approaches
- Generated a pleasing template for customer letters
- Has a good eye for colors
- Has developed a number of creative solutions
- Generated a number of creative solutions for clients

Needs Improvement
- Prefers the tried and true over radically different ideas
- Lacks creativity
- Rarely has new ideas
- Could strengthen ability to see what's not there
- Needs to be more open to others' ideas
- Tends to be staid in thinking outside the box
- Ideas lack sparkle and pizzazz
- Mostly modifies others' ideas, rarely generates them
- Our clients rarely accept his ideas
- Had few suggestions while on the Quick Start Committee

Unacceptable
- Creativity far below what job requires
- Unimaginative
- Formats tend to be unstylish and dull
- Sees only what's there, not what's not
- Lacks the level of creativity required
- Does not suggest creative solutions to problems
- Fearful of the new and different
- Has not solved any old problems
- Locked into tried and true, not new
- Never contributes a creative idea
- Clients have not accepted ideas

Customer Relations

Outstanding
- Relates to customers exceedingly well
- Has developed an incredibly loyal customer base
- Wonderful at customer relations
- Resourceful in finding solutions to problems
- Always delivers on promises
- It's no wonder we have as many happy customers as we do
- Relates well to corporate and individual customers

Exceeds Expectations
- Has won us customer loyalty many times
- Graceful and tactful under pressure from customers
- Customer relations a strength
- Always patient, competent, and professional with customers
- Solves customer problems with speed and accuracy
- Represents our company very well

Meets Expectations
- Usually competent and professional with customers
- An able representative
- Courteous and knowledgeable
- Professional presentation
- Manages all but the most challenging customer situations
- Handles customer relations responsibilities well

Needs Improvement
- Gets annoyed by customers with a lot of questions
- Sometimes gets sarcastic
- Presents a sloppy and uncaring image

- Customer relation skills need improvement
- On several occasions has lost temper with customers
- Conducts personal phone conversations while customers wait

Unacceptable
- Frequently impolite
- Very weak customer relation skills
- Condescends to customers
- Ignores customers
- Chews gum while speaking with customers
- Shouted obscenities at a customer

Data Entry

Outstanding
- Extremely fast and accurate
- In top 5% for data entry
- Always willing to take on complicated projects
- Enters data for long periods while maintaining excellent accuracy

Exceeds Expectations
- Is very fast and accurate
- Always enters in proper fields
- Enters correct data in correct fields
- Has good stamina in working through a large amount of data
- Can enter _____ characters in _____ minutes

Meets Expectations
- Correctly enters data
- Takes and enters data correctly from customers
- Maintains good accuracy and speed
- Proofs while entering
- Completes data entry within expected time limits

Needs Improvement
- Is slower than most, with lower-than-average accuracy
- Slow at keying data
- Can't touch-type numbers
- Enters data incorrectly regularly
- Puts data in incorrect fields

Unacceptable
- Data entries contain an unacceptable amount of errors
- Frequently makes mistakes in data entry

- Doesn't catch entry errors
- Doesn't put data in proper fields
- Takes 2 hours where the standard entry time is 30 minutes

Deadlines, Ability to Meet

Outstanding
- Consistently ahead of schedule
- Volunteers to work with tight deadlines
- Quickly gets and stays on task
- Completed tasks on time when nobody else could

Exceeds Expectations
- Able to block out distractions
- Amazing task focus when needed
- Seems to thrive on pressure deadlines
- Maintains quality with tight timelines

Meets Expectations
- Generally delivers on time
- Meets deadlines well in periods of calm
- Requires little supervision in tough deadline situations
- Informs when delays anticipated

Needs Improvement
- Missed deadlines more than once this year
- Lack of organization skills sometimes causes delays
- Needs to be more independent to meet deadlines
- Hesitant to take on tough deadlines
- Flustered when deadlines changed

Unacceptable
- Often misses standard deadlines
- Cannot handle any short-deadline tasks or assignments
- Job may be too pressure-packed
- Not suited to any short-deadline work
- Doesn't admit to being behind schedule

Decision Making

Outstanding

- Clearly understands the implications of situations and uses sound judgment when deciding what to do
- Makes tough decisions
- Decisions always appropriate
- Weighs options carefully and thoroughly
- Can decide in the most challenging situations
- Will make decisions about major issues
- Can always be counted on to make good decisions when faced with a dilemma
- Decisions take into account the needs of all stakeholders

Exceeds Expectations

- Will make decision when others are afraid to commit to a course of action
- Analytic and decisive
- Decisions are well thought out
- Considers "human cost" in decisions
- Decisions always result of detailed analysis
- Makes decisions quickly and appropriately
- Involves others in decision making

Meets Expectations

- Usually makes appropriate decisions
- Gathers ample information to make reasoned decision
- Considers many alternatives
- Involves others appropriately when making decisions
- Bases decisions on facts not personalities
- Communicates decisions clearly and directly

Needs Improvement

- Delays making necessary decisions

- Often comes to management for help with a decision
- Sticks with status quo rather than make a decision
- Uses gut rather than facts for decision making
- Always accepts others' decisions

Unacceptable
- Extremely fearful of making a mistake
- Logic fails in decision making
- Often fails to see problems that require decisions
- Fails to gather necessary information for decision making
- Frequently makes bad decisions
- Never makes a decision
- Avoids decision-making situations

Dedication to Job/Work

Outstanding

- Is a "go-getter" in the best sense of the term
- Completes extensive research on potential clients before making a sales call
- Is focused on all projects
- Exceptionally dedicated
- Works overtime whenever asked
- Extremely dedicated and committed
- Follows directions precisely
- Questions unclear instructions
- Three days out of five, works until 8:00 p.m. to complete tasks

Exceeds Expectations

- Assumes personal responsibility
- Very committed
- Does whatever's necessary to satisfy customers
- Always shows a "can do" attitude
- Routinely works late
- Learns about new technologies affecting work
- Often skips breaks in order to minimize backlogs
- Came in on two Saturdays for extra practice
- Studies user manuals to gain greater skills in our database program

Meets Expectations

- Keeps promises
- Dedicated to goals
- Obeys policies
- Requested training to advance computer skills
- Shows pride in work

- Works regularly scheduled hours
- Completes work well enough to pass minimum standards

Needs Improvement
- Doesn't adhere to team goals
- Lacks commitment
- Rarely manifests real dedication
- Does the least required
- Leaves rework for next shift
- Often fails to follow directions
- Frequently engages in personal phone calls

Unacceptable
- Doesn't keep current on projects
- Apathetic about performance improvement
- His/Her work is very slow and inaccurate
- Works only when given a warning
- Leaves work for client undone at end of day
- Recommended a competitor's product during a customer service call
- Missed __ out of __ team meetings

Delegation

Outstanding

- Direct reports gained considerable skill through delegated responsibilities
- Delegates appropriate and challenging responsibilities
- Has strengthened department considerably through effective delegation
- Gives employees energizing and challenging assignments
- Always follows up on results of delegated projects
- Has divided the department's work among five task forces

Exceeds Expectations

- Frequently passes assignments from upper management to able staff members
- Uses delegation to develop staff
- Allows staff to take authority to fulfill responsibilities
- Keeps staff energized with new projects
- Rarely delegates menial tasks
- Creates challenging projects to delegate

Meets Expectations

- Usually keeps workload manageable by enlisting help
- Delegates responsibility with required authority
- Considers staff's capabilities before delegating
- Mixes the mundane and challenging
- Delegates fairly

Needs Improvement

- Fails to check on progress of delegated assignments
- Needs to delegate more challenging assignments

- Fails to give clear directions or goals when delegating
- Stockpiles projects, waiting for time to complete them
- Makes many needless changes in others' work

Unacceptable

- Never delegates and is far behind schedule
- Doesn't consider employees' capabilities when assigning work
- Delegates without direction or support
- Does all complex, challenging projects
- Has failed to meet goals because of lack of delegation

Dependability

Outstanding

- Willingly takes accountability for all departmental activities
- Can always be counted on to complete assignments
- Always delivers on promises
- Highest level of dependability
- Achieves results with minimal resources
- Always achieves stated goals and more
- Assumes personal responsibility for his/her work
- Performs work independently and accurately
- Takes action and makes decisions quickly
- Always delivers on time
- Followed up personally with over __ customers

Exceeds Expectations

- Delivers on promises far more than not
- High level of accountability for projects
- Does not disappoint when deadlines are tight
- Almost always adheres to instructions/directions
- Performs most work independently
- Delivered __ of __ completed reports on time
- Missed only __ days of work in last year

Meets Expectations

- Appropriate level of accountability
- Delivers on promises
- Adheres to policies and guidelines
- Conscientious worker
- Accountable for projects
- Follows directions and instructions
- Needs little oversight on projects

➡

Needs Improvement

- Fails to accept accountability for missed deadlines
- Does not accept accountability for project failures
- Frequently fails to achieve goals
- Does not follow directions or instructions
- Needs oversight
- Doesn't take action or make decisions without direction
- Has missed deadlines __ times
- Returned late from breaks __ times in the year

Unacceptable

- Fails to ever accept accountability for own behavior or results
- Always attributes failure to others or circumstances
- Rarely delivers a project on time
- Does not achieve agreed upon goals
- Frequently does not follow directions or instructions
- Needs constant oversight
- Rarely takes action or makes decisions without guidance or direction
- Needs frequent reminders to keep projects on track
- Arrived late __ out of __ days in __ weeks
- Uses the phone for personal conversations

Development of Subordinates

Outstanding
- Exceedingly devoted to staff development
- Creative and dedicated to developing others
- Training and delegation combine to develop an excellent staff
- Always registers new employees for appropriate training
- Inspires staff to learn
- Always shares relevant company information with subordinates

Exceeds Expectations
- Invests time during all appraisals on personal development
- Has an "open door" to new employees who have questions about the job
- Reinforces and supports new employee orientation
- Uses delegation well to develop staff
- Excellent role model for continuous learning

Meets Expectations
- Gives employees advanced training and additional responsibilities
- Develops employees appropriately
- Regularly shares management information during staff meetings
- Every employee in the department received training in Excel

Needs Improvement
- Insufficient training has led to poor productivity
- Fails to develop staff in needed areas

- Does not appropriately develop staff to perform needed duties
- Her department suffered a 10% error rate due to inadequate training

Unacceptable
- Staff is poorly trained
- Delegates only menial tasks
- Error rate in department is unacceptable
- Received numerous customer complaints about staff's capability and courtesy
- Has repeatedly delayed giving new employees orientation to the department

Equal Opportunity/Diversity

Outstanding
- An excellent model of EEO practices
- Invites diverse ideas
- Ensures staff represents percentage of protected classes in population
- Sensitive to and respectful of all individuals
- Formed a task force to attract minority achievers

Exceeds Expectations
- Provides equal opportunities to members of protected classes
- Is free of bias in personnel evaluations
- Maintains pay equity for all staff in similar positions
- Ensures that staff from disadvantaged backgrounds receive appropriate training

Meets Expectations
- Bases all personnel decisions on performance
- Supports EEO and diversity values
- Shows no indication of bias
- Makes decisions based on performance, not personal characteristics
- Has hired from diverse ethnic backgrounds

Needs Improvement
- Needs to strengthen EEO/diversity orientation
- Has only white males in supervisory positions
- Members of protected classes and women are paid less
- Minorities enrolled in fewer training sessions
- Department lacks ethnic diversity

Unacceptable
- Has blatantly discriminated

- Will not interview minority candidates
- Has told off-color jokes in staff meetings
- Minorities consistently receive lower performance ratings
- Several lawsuits cite his failure to promote Hispanic workers despite their merit

Ethical Behavior

Outstanding
- Exceptionally scrupulous and honest in all activities
- Does what's right regardless of consequences
- Always demonstrates integrity and honesty
- Is exceptionally conscientious in potential conflict of interest situations
- Has received high praise for swift and generous remedies for product defects
- Has retained or gained new customers due to honesty

Exceeds Expectations
- Never lies or bends the truth
- Argues vigorously for fair dealing
- Created a clear values statement for staff about ethics
- Knows and follows applicable laws
- Customers have been happily surprised by honesty

Meets Expectations
- Deals with customers fairly
- Will not exploit loopholes in laws for benefit
- Staff understands and follows ethical guidelines
- Is noted for honesty and fairness

Needs Improvement
- Sometimes sees ethics as an inconvenience
- Has been known to stretch the law for gain
- Has behaved unethically in dealings with clients
- Complaints have been lodged about this store's bait-and-switch tactics

Unacceptable
- Does not behave ethically

➡

- Has lied to others in department
- Violates our ethical guidelines
- The state's attorney general has initiated legal action
- Actions have resulted in customers refusing to do business with us

Feedback, Receiving and Giving

Outstanding
- Always offers criticism in a constructive manner
- Consistently receives feedback constructively
- Involves staff in deciding how to improve work output and quality
- Initiates changes based on all feedback appropriately
- Welcomes feedback, especially negative

Exceeds Expectations
- Delivers feedback in a sensitive and caring way
- Translates criticism into positive changes
- Seeks to understand rather than defend against negative feedback
- Explains feedback to institute behavioral changes
- Accepts all negative feedback positively

Meets Expectations
- Usually is receptive to feedback and appreciative
- Provides feedback to subordinates as necessary
- Works to learn from feedback received
- Delivers negative comments to staff while maintaining positive relations
- Can turn most criticism into appropriate action

Needs Improvement
- Is often silent when constructive criticism is called for
- Will criticize the person and not his or her actions
- Delivers negative feedback in a personally hurtful manner
- Tends to deliver feedback in an insensitive way
- Disagrees with constructive criticism, rather than accepting

Unacceptable

- Never offers criticism in a constructive manner
- Consistently receives feedback defensively and argumentatively
- Consistently shies away from providing necessary feedback
- Does not speak with staff about how to improve work output and quality
- Consistently takes feedback with negativity and disagreement

Financial Management

Outstanding
- Anticipates financial problems before they occur
- Provided meaningful information to decision makers
- Involves staff in financial improvement initiatives
- Implements prudent risk analysis

Exceeds Expectations
- Gets the most from scarce resources
- Implemented measures for financial accountability
- Uses accounting information to make decisions
- Actual expenditures within 10% of budget projections

Meets Expectations
- Understands and uses standard accounting practices
- Prepares budget projections on time
- Translates raw financial data into information for others
- Follows standard financial practices
- Stays current on financial issues during year
- Prepares appropriate year-end statements
- Accurately reports financial status

Needs Improvement
- Exceeded budget by 20% last year
- Loses financial big picture
- Could control expenditures better
- Difficult to understand "the books"
- Financial reports tend to gloss over bad news

Unacceptable
- Often runs in deficit mode
- Uncooperative with company auditors
- Does not inform superiors of potential problems

- Has ignored serious accounting errors
- Financial reports are intentionally misleading
- Does not accept responsibility for financial problems

Flexibility

Outstanding
- When asked to work unusual hours, always complies
- Is among the most flexible members of our team
- Drops current work to promptly address emergencies
- Shifted from the 8-4 shift to the midnight-8 shift when requested without complaint

Exceeds Expectations
- Has mastered different approaches to situations and can flexibly respond when it's required
- Able to shift focus rapidly
- Willingly assumes others' tasks in case of absences
- Accommodates others' needs first

Meets Expectations
- Gracefully accepts changes to work
- Will reset priorities as required
- Adjusts to changes in procedure fairly well
- Often changes schedule to meet production deadlines

Needs Improvement
- Resists changes
- Argues against resetting priorities
- Becomes agitated when asked to work outside the daily routine
- Frequently will not change mind, despite new evidence

Unacceptable
- Lacks flexibility in most situations
- Won't make changes in priorities until disciplined
- Failure to shift priorities has lost us two clients

General Job Skills

Outstanding
- Mastered every aspect of job
- Exceptional in every skill required on this job
- Rapidly created folders and subfolders for extremely complex document database
- Exceptional organizational ability
- Learned and applied new software within two weeks

Exceeds Expectations
- Has natural ability to quickly comprehend instruction and apply new skills
- Performs efficiently and well
- Quickly adapted to new software
- Created a database comprising over 500 separate documents

Meets Expectations
- Performs tasks competently
- Usually meets deadlines
- Needs strengthening in just a few areas
- Is skilled in most aspects of job

Needs Improvement
- Needs repeated instruction when learning new tasks
- Needs to improve a few fundamental skills
- Has the ability to learn, but seems disinterested in gaining proficiency
- Needed to repeat training for intermediate applications

Unacceptable
- Must improve job skills for satisfactory performance

➡

- Unable to perform a number of functions within standards
- Errors in work often exceed standards
- Time to complete tasks often exceeds standards
- His work contains three times as many errors as the average

Goal Achievement

Outstanding
- The larger the challenge, the more effort
- Achieved goals that others have failed
- In an emergency the person to rely on
- Achieves goals, then looks for more

Exceeds Expectations
- Overcomes frustrating circumstances to achieve goals
- Juggles various goals and achieves most of them
- Doesn't get thrown by tough situations
- Removes barriers to goal achievement
- Does not let everyday problems deflect focus from goals

Meets Expectations
- Meets goals on time
- Takes responsibility for goal achievement
- Comfortable being held accountable for achievement
- Informs others when problems occur
- Helps teammates achieve goals

Needs Improvement
- Goal achievement suffers under pressure
- Lack of confidence sometimes interferes with achievement
- Needs to work on achieving several goals at once

Unacceptable
- Consistently unable to achieve even basic goals
- Doesn't seem to care about reaching goals
- Denies failure to achieve goals
- Makes excuses when goals not attained
- Blames others

Goal and Objective Setting

Outstanding
- Basically self-directing
- Goals she/he sets are always relevant to organization big picture
- Seems to automatically know what must be achieved
- Always seems clear about what to do
- Often asks questions that help the group clarify goals

Exceeds Expectations
- Coaches others in setting sensible goals
- Good at phrasing objectives
- Communicates objectives and goals effectively
- Understands link between goals and planning tasks
- Skilled at mapping out goals and plans of action

Meets Expectations
- Accepts goals set out by supervisor
- Goals chosen are realistic
- Achieves most goals assigned
- Alters goal priorities as needed
- Is guided by goals and objectives

Needs Improvement
- Could show more initiative in setting own goals
- Often asks others what to do next
- Hesitant to work with manager to set goals
- Sets vague or unmeasurable objectives
- Goals and objectives need to be examined by supervisor

Unacceptable
- Sets goals impossible to achieve
- Unaware of organization goals and objectives

- Has no interest in setting goals
- Pays no attention to objectives
- Doesn't make the link between goals and job success
- Just wants to do his/her own thing
- Sets goals way under capabilities

Grooming and Appearance

Outstanding
- Impeccable dress and grooming
- By appearance, represents our company extremely well
- Immaculate appearance
- Immediately conveys positive impression
- Fashionable, yet understated appearance
- Projects a very positive image for company

Exceeds Expectations
- A polished appearance
- Appears composed and professional
- Appears, and is, knowledgeable and confident
- Dresses properly for all business occasions

Meets Expectations
- Comes to work properly attired
- Meets all our guidelines for grooming and appearance
- Carries himself/herself with confidence
- Clothes are clean and pressed
- Shows a professional image

Needs Improvement
- Grooming and appearance need to be improved
- Lacks expression and enthusiasm
- Often has a sloppy appearance
- Pants and shirt are often mismatched
- Others have asked to be seated far away from him/her

Unacceptable
- Ignored requests to deal with appearance
- Will often underdress for important meetings
- Disheveled and unclean appearance

➡

- Shows a poor image of our company
- Clothes are often dirty and wrinkled
- Some have reported unpleasant body odor

Initiative

Outstanding
- Always seeking ways to show initiative
- Knows when and how to take action
- Shows strong initiative in every situation
- Worked an extra ___ hours to eliminate error messages in database
- Developed a new work process for communications between accounting and marketing
- Foresaw crisis with client X and express-shipped part to ensure they had no work stoppage—client praised her
- Called together representatives from three departments and solved problem with client X

Exceeds Expectations
- Takes initiative frequently and appropriately
- Is above the norm in showing initiative
- Does not shy away from taking risks
- Without instruction, negotiated lower rates with ___ of ___ vendors
- Redesigned existing software to solve serious customer problem

Meets Expectations
- Takes initiative when appropriate
- Comfortable making decisions to solve customers' problems
- Likes limits specifically spelled out, but goes to them willingly
- Will take risks to accommodate customers
- Created a project oversight committee and its mission statement with minimal direction

➡

- Instituted extranet connection for vendor X to improve project coordination
- Can take initiative when called for

Needs Improvement
- Does only what's asked
- Slow to act
- Rarely shows initiative
- Doesn't make decisions without approval
- Failed to solve customer X's problem
- Not yet confident enough to make decisions
- Shows initiative at a level below what the job requires

Unacceptable
- Shows initiative at a level far below that which is required by the job
- Displays no initiative
- No independent action
- Waits until directed to act
- Delays decisions until it's too late
- Lost a large customer because of lack of initiative
- Takes no initiative to solve customers' problems

Interpersonal Skills

Outstanding
- Often requested as a work partner
- Excellent conflict management skills
- Managers call this person a breeze to work with
- Effective interacting with people no matter the status
- Relates to everyone well regardless of their background
- Genuinely interested

Exceeds Expectations
- Seeks first to understand
- Corrects others without being offensive
- Assertive but doesn't offend
- Open to improving interpersonal skills
- Accepts people from other cultures
- Is accepted by people from other cultures

Meets Expectations
- Does not make sexist or racist comments
- Sense of humor appropriate
- Gets along OK in most situations
- Communicates with others well
- A little awkward in some social situations
- Manages own anger well

Needs Improvement
- Doesn't always listen carefully
- Quick to lose patience
- Sometimes tells inappropriate jokes
- Doesn't use skills in emotionally charged situations
- Body language and words don't always match
- Some believe tone is arrogant

➡

Unacceptable
- Often makes insensitive criticisms of others
- Talks behind people's backs
- Received justified complaints from coworkers
- Has not benefited from coaching
- Consistently passive-aggressive
- Tries to look good by attacking others

Judgment

Outstanding

- Shows strong judgment in the most difficult situations
- Excels at balancing risk and reward
- A thorough, thoughtful analyst of complicated scenarios
- Helped company avert a costly strike through skillful negotiation
- Has clear understanding of the implications of decisions

Exceeds Expectations

- Demonstrates mature, seasoned judgment
- Made good decisions in a number of difficult cases
- Interceded effectively in a number of "political" clashes
- Makes decisions based on facts and interests of the organization

Meets Expectations

- Examines different sides of situations prior to making a decision
- Shows clear judgment in resolving conflict
- Elevated customers' concerns to executive-level contact, appropriately
- Strengthened relationship with accounting by authorizing overtime to complete project X on time

Needs Improvement

- Sometimes shows poor judgment in dealing with his/her staff
- Needs to "consider the source" more when judging situations
- Finds it difficult to be nonjudgmental when judgment dictates it
- Needs to strengthen situational awareness

Unacceptable

- Has lacked sound judgment on a number of critical occasions
- Doesn't verify information before forming judgments
- Has shown poor judgment in a number of client interactions
- Got into a shouting match with a VP at a board meeting
- Poor decisions resulted in lowered group performance

Knowledge of Company Processes

Outstanding
- His/her knowledge is unsurpassed
- Knows the organization inside out
- Has been nominated to three cross-functional teams
- Excellent person to answer questions about company
- Applied knowledge to improve company-wide processes
- Has identified process problems others have missed

Exceeds Expectations
- Understands the influences on decision making very well
- Serves as liaison to marketing, sales, and manufacturing
- Uses knowledge of big picture to guide action

Meets Expectations
- Sufficiently understands processes
- Knows interactions between his/her function and others in department
- Understands finance and marketing well, but needs more background on manufacturing
- Changed label location so shipping could find it easier

Needs Improvement
- Is still learning our workflow
- Unfamiliar with a few basic processes
- Still learning his/her way around
- Needs to learn about our clients' expectations of us

Unacceptable
- Is unfamiliar with how his/her function affects others
- Makes changes without checking with those they affect
- Doesn't understand the link between sales and development
- Repeated two past failures because of lack of research

Knowledge of Job

Outstanding

- Has complete mastery of his/her job
- Has a great wealth of knowledge about all job facets
- Her level of knowledge is outstanding
- His is an expert in the functioning of system X
- Has authoritative understanding of job responsibilities
- Is source of information for others in department
- Has kept XYZ certification current for 10 years in a row
- Gained certification in XYZ-2.0 this year

Exceeds Expectations

- Understands all aspects of job
- Strong level of job knowledge
- Knowledge exceeds what is required to perform well

Meets Expectations

- Level of job knowledge appropriate to perform tasks require
- Understands X and Y very well
- Maintains knowledge through seminars and courses
- Knows most of the systems necessary to succeed
- Keeps up to date through reading industry periodicals

Needs Improvement

- Needs to learn more to perform job satisfactorily
- Often runs into situations where he doesn't know what to do
- Is out of date with knowledge
- Needs to improve job knowledge
- Infrequently has the job knowledge to know what to do
- Needs to ask for help on many projects
- Makes more errors than average

Unacceptable

- Needs to learn much more to perform job satisfactorily
- Is many years out of date with knowledge
- Rarely has the job knowledge to know what to do
- Needs to ask for help on every project
- Makes many more errors than average

Leadership Skills

Outstanding

- Uses participative approach whenever called for
- Clearly understands leading as facilitating the success of team and company
- Has employees fired up and committed to organizational goals and vision
- Turns on the motivation for excellence among employees
- Persevered through many leadership challenges
- Excellent at training, motivating, and guiding staff
- Builds excellent team spirit and direction
- Takes all blame, shares all successes
- Employees show great loyalty
- Ranked as superior leader by __ of __ subordinates
- Led group to exceed sales targets in __ of __ regions
- Championed movement to ERP system-migration, completed __ months ahead of target

Exceeds Expectations

- Has the confidence of employees and peers
- Has a participative approach
- Organizes teams with insight into talents and capabilities
- Demeanor sets an example for others
- Considers staff's personal and professional welfare
- Assertive and firm, while fair
- Has authority but leads without dictating
- Dedicates the time and effort necessary to achieve results
- Willing to make tough decisions
- Exhibits traits that generate confidence
- Headed numerous successful projects

Meets Expectations

- Effectively motivates and directs
- Leads staff
- Holds and displays company values
- Satisfactorily overcame some leadership challenges
- Shows strengths in leading, motivating, coaching
- Sits as equal team member on many committees
- Puts worker safety above productivity
- Encourages others to share ideas and approaches
- Could become an excellent leader someday
- Is a developing leader; strong in some areas already

Needs Improvement

- Isn't secure about being in front
- Needs to develop leadership characteristics
- Sometimes fails to inform staff of changes
- Will sometimes put productivity ahead of staff welfare and safety
- Rarely gets involved to resolve disputes among employees
- Needs to ask what others think more often
- Led well, but not in the right direction
- Sets unrealistic goals
- Rarely involves staff in decision making

Unacceptable

- Dictates rather than lead
- Appears totally unable to build teams and direct others' activities
- Doesn't command authority
- Fails to train, motivate, or direct staff
- Will not solicit opinions from others
- Takes over all meetings attended

➡

- Has minimized safety concerns to meet production goals
- Sets goals contrary to company mission
- Fails to act in complex situations
- Never involves others in making decisions
- Is usually late in giving staff vital information
- Behavior generates frequent employee complaints
- Has lost respect of employees

Listening Skills

Outstanding
- Listens and understands even when upset
- Creates a climate where staff listens to each other
- Able to empathize with other's situations
- Manages to appear attentive even in difficult situations

Exceeds Expectations
- Accurately interprets what is said
- Makes frequent use of active or reflective listening
- Only needs to be told once
- Honestly interested in what others say

Meets Expectations
- Understands and can use active/reflective listening
- Follows directions accurately
- Questions when unsure of understanding
- Remembers what others have said over time

Needs Improvement
- Doesn't use listening skills in "tough" situations
- Sometimes so anxious to speak that he/she stops listening
- Needs things explained several times
- Sometimes distracted by own thoughts

Unacceptable
- Constantly interrupts
- Often misinterprets due to bias
- Poor attention span
- Drifts off during important meetings when not speaking
- Not aware when she/he doesn't understand

Long-Range Planning

Outstanding

- Shows great foresight
- An exceedingly strong strategic planner
- Developed a cost-cutting plan that avoided mandatory layoffs
- Makes use of long-range plans in everyday decision making

Exceeds Expectations

- Always looking three to five years down the road
- Anticipated decline in sector and identified three new markets for our product
- Links long-term planning to shorter-term implementation

Meets Expectations

- Has planned for contingencies well
- A good tactical planner
- Identified need and developed an Internet browsing workshop

Needs Improvement

- Needs to look further down the road
- Good with tactics but needs to strengthen strategic plans

Unacceptable

- Has been caught off guard repeatedly by market changes
- Ten-year plan skips the first three years
- Plans long term then ignores it

Management Control

Outstanding
- Able to track multiple issues and problems
- Identifies problems before they occur
- Shares control with employees
- Views control as a means for improving processes
- Expert in the use of statistical process control
- Takes action to prevent problems early in process

Exceeds Expectations
- Manages changing priorities
- Does not overextend by overinvolvement
- Chooses staff wisely to take control of responsibilities
- Regularly looks for ways to improve the system

Meets Expectations
- Provides an adequate level of management control
- Unit tends to run smoothly
- Attends to details when needed

Needs Improvement
- Seeks to control everything, negatively affecting productivity
- Could exercise greater control
- Staff takes advantage of flexibility
- Sometimes relies on wrong people
- Failed to know that a staff member would be absent from a critical meeting

Unacceptable
- Consistently out of touch with work going on
- Exercises minimal control over staff
- Seen by others as hoarding power

- Unable to make fast decisions
- Allows problems to go on too long
- Crises regularly occur in his/her area of responsibility

Management Skills

Outstanding
- Delegates effectively
- Keeps employees in the loop
- An excellent planner
- Organizes people and resources for efficiency and success
- Stays informed without being intrusive
- Uses time and resources effectively
- Strong at screening and hiring new employees
- Effectively handles employee conflicts
- Helps others take responsibility and action

Exceeds Expectations
- Models desired behavior for staff
- Mastered and uses basic coaching skills
- Rarely needs to use formal disciplinary action
- Processes normally operate well with few problems
- Plans well

Meets Expectations
- Maintains personnel and financial records as required
- Plans normally have few glitches
- Regularly informs superiors of progress/problems
- Usually achieves goals and objectives
- Effective participant in hiring process

Needs Improvement
- Micromanages many employee activities
- Has used threats to move employees
- Employee turnover rate higher than the average
- Employee sick time higher than average without reason
- Does not understand how to plan

➡

- New hires often don't work out

Unacceptable
- Takes credit for staff accomplishments
- Plans poorly and problems often occur as result
- Makes poor use of time
- Processes poorly organized
- Often confronts project crises
- Work often finished late and over budget
- Been subject of more than one successful grievance in last 12 months

Managing Details

Outstanding
- Can communicate details to others
- Translates big picture to impact on details
- Breaks down problems into manageable detail
- Makes sure the small things get done well

Exceeds Expectations
- Does not get overwhelmed by details
- Keeps big picture in mind at all times
- Delegates details to best people

Meets Expectations
- Knows when to tend to detail and when not
- Communicates regularly with others involved in detail work
- Seeks help when overwhelmed
- Documents details so others can track

Needs Improvement
- Sometimes loses track of things or misses steps
- Can't identify details of simple problems
- Stress levels rise as detail complexity increases

Unacceptable
- Easily bored with small details
- Many details fall through cracks
- Short attention span causes problems
- Overwhelmed by more than simple details

Managing Expenses

Outstanding
- Does not inflate budget spending estimates
- Often comes in under budget
- Purchases only what is needed for success
- Sets priorities for spending to increase productivity

Exceeds Expectations
- Does not impede necessary small expenditures
- Provides staff with reasonable spending authority
- Teaches staff to link spending with results
- Has developed new lower-cost methods now used in company

Meets Expectations
- Completes expenditure reports on time
- Stays within budget except for emergency situations
- Timely responses to queries about expenditures
- Seeks out cost-effective options

Needs Improvement
- Many unplanned purchases made unnecessarily
- Chronically inflates expenses during planning
- Takes a competitive attitude during budgeting

Unacceptable
- Return on investment for expenditures is low
- Approves and makes purchases impulsively
- Lobbies for unneeded staff and money
- Has used money for purposes other than allocated

Mechanical Skills

Outstanding
- Superior mechanical skills
- Can fix every piece of machinery in the shop
- Works precisely, quickly, and safely
- Has engineered a number of improvements
- Repairs fine mechanical pieces
- An excellent troubleshooter

Exceeds Expectations
- Has troubleshot many mechanical failures
- Repairs most devices without assistance
- Makes delicate repairs
- Problem solves failures quickly
- Consistently within time standards for jobs

Meets Expectations
- Able to repair most common problems with machinery
- An able and safe mechanic
- Competent at mechanical operations
- Know where to find information if needed
- Meets standards for mechanical procedures
- Shows ample strength and dexterity for the job
- Adequate eye-hand coordination

Needs Improvement
- Slow at troubleshooting
- Shortcuts procedures to save time
- Lacks coordination to operate machine X
- Needs to improve understanding of the internal mechanism
- Mistakes hardware problems for software problems

Unacceptable

- Generally poor mechanical skills
- Works slowly and without regard for safety procedures
- Has sacrificed safety for quantity
- Needs oversight on most mechanical operations
- Hasn't diagnosed root cause for machine X's failure
- Unable to operate machine X after ____ months of training

Multi-Tasking

Outstanding
- Manages many projects at the same time effortlessly
- Has met milestones for all four major projects
- Managed $14.7M worth of projects across three clients
- Uses project management software very effectively

Exceeds Expectations
- Can separate different aspects of her work very well
- Consistently maintains project management log for 13 projects
- Delegated high-level, challenging responsibilities to subordinates while maintaining oversight

Meets Expectations
- Has ably handled multiple tasks
- Can move from one task to another competently
- Usually completes a variety of tasks within needed timeframes
- Capable of coordinating two project teams' needs simultaneously

Needs Improvement
- Could strengthen concentration when working on many tasks
- Has fumbled one or two assignments requiring a number of tasks
- Forgets to do minor tasks that have cost us time later
- Capably coordinates one meeting, but can't handle two at the same time

Unacceptable
- Things often fall through the cracks when he/she has many responsibilities

- Loses focus when faced with even minor additional assignments
- Has walked out of the office on three occasions, frustrated with an average workload
- Fails to remember or write down essential tasks

Negotiating Skills

Outstanding
- Always negotiates successful win-win agreements
- Negotiated agreements that resulted in ___ new projects for company
- Contractees consistently positive about negotiation process
- Does not make agreements that aren't in the company's interests
- Agreements bring positive results for company
- Legal always signs off on agreements
- Takes into consideration needs of all stakeholders

Exceeds Expectations
- Most negotations go smoothly
- Legal seldom questions agreements
- Contractees happy with agreements
- Takes into consideration most contingencies
- Agreements usually profitable for company

Meets Expectations
- Can be trusted to negotiate in company's interests
- Makes use of legal advice during negotiation
- Informs superiors of progress on negotiations
- Takes others' views into account
- Agreements usually succeed
- Uses reason rather than emotion in negotiations

Needs Improvement
- Does not adequately understand the give-and-take of negotiation
- Sometimes gets emotional during a negotiation
- Sometimes gives more than received

➡

- Not well prepared in some negotiation sessions

Unacceptable
- Consistently tries to take advantage of others
- Does not prepare for negotiation sessions
- Negotiations often result in loss for company
- Often gets emotional while negotiating
- Is unaware of contingencies in an agreement
- Agreements more often lose-lose than win-win

Organizing Skills

Outstanding
- Completed a major reorganizing project this year
- Others rely on him/her to help stay organized
- Taught others organizating skills last year
- Always on top of things

Exceeds Expectations
- Others can find things she/he organizes
- Has customer information at tip of fingers
- Stays organized under high stress
- Keeps track of multiple things at once

Meets Expectations
- Keeps workspace functional
- Keeps well organized files
- Can find needed information
- Uses organizing tools to save time (e.g., to-do list)

Needs Improvement
- Requires a long time to find documents
- Filing system not easy for others to use
- Sometimes too concerned with neatness
- Intolerant of organizing approaches of others
- Could be more tolerant of others' disorganization

Unacceptable
- Often loses things
- Has missed meetings due to disorganization
- Offends customers due to losing things
- Often fails to file important documents
- Wastes time because of missing items

Orientation to Work

Outstanding

- Keeps job in proper perspective
- Helps team members be more productive
- Completes the toughest assignments
- Has all skills required for excellent work
- Joy to work with

Exceeds Expectations

- Volunteers more than others
- Quick to learn from mistakes
- Interested in learning new things
- Concerned with team members' success

Meets Expectations

- Takes pride in work
- Balances needs of job and family
- Treats customers well
- Always on time

Needs Improvement

- Avoids leadership opportunities
- Sometimes anxious about new challenges
- Sometimes too cautious
- Easily distracted by non-work issues

Unacceptable

- Seems uninterested in doing well
- Last to volunteer for work assignments
- Refuses to pitch in during emergencies
- Overly pessimistic
- Lacks skills required to perform acceptably

Participative Management

Outstanding
- Knows when to delegate and not to delegate
- Inspires others to have confidence in themselves
- Identifies and uses employees' strengths and knowledge
- Understands own limitations
- Open to employee criticisms

Exceeds Expectations
- Employees comfortable making suggestions
- Gets staff input for major decisions
- Helps staff understand the company's business
- Provides open-door access that employees use

Meets Expectations
- Delegates, then does not meddle
- Treats employee input seriously
- Provides needed information to staff
- Rewards staff for good ideas

Needs Improvement
- Pretends to delegate but stays too involved
- Sometimes defensive
- Prefers autocratic style
- Staff hesitant to approach with ideas

Unacceptable
- Employees afraid to become involved
- Intimidates staff
- Asks for suggestions, then ignores
- Takes credit for employees' ideas
- Negative attitude undermines cooperation among

Personal Growth

Outstanding
- Balances work and family/outside interests
- Independently pursues opportunities to learn
- Demonstrates continuous learning
- Has pursued mentor relationship

Exceeds Expectations
- Dramatic improvement in maturity over last two years
- Improved stress management ability this year
- Seeks to improve understanding of diverse people
- Helps others with personal growth

Meets Expectations
- Seeks help as needed
- Assumes responsibility for own successes/failures
- Regularly asks for feedback and responds by making an effort to improve
- Sees problems as opportunity to learn

Needs Improvement
- Overly sensitive to negative feedback
- Seems to have reached a "growth plateau"
- Goes into denial when faced with personal problems
- Work negatively impacted by personal issues

Unacceptable
- Denies existence of personal difficulties
- Refuses needed help
- Has unresolved substance abuse problems
- Prone to self-deception
- Work suffers because of inability to balance work, family, and outside interests

Persuasiveness

Outstanding

- Captures minds and hearts
- Understands and believes in the problem-solving approach in convincing others
- Makes excellent use of "shared benefits" to influence
- Makes sales others cannot
- When she/he speaks, others want to listen
- Other leaves believing idea was own

Exceeds Expectations

- Anticipates others' needs and wants
- Modifies communication to reach different audiences
- Excellent timing of persuasive messages
- Effective in responding to objections
- Speaks with power
- Confident speaking to large groups

Meets Expectations

- Justifies position logically
- References supporting information
- Can adequately answer questions
- Does not "oversell"
- Writes coherent, persuasive documents as needed
- Seen as helpful during persuasion efforts

Needs Improvement

- Sometimes timid
- Doesn't realize merit of own ideas
- Not always aware of how she/he comes across
- Lacks some large group speaking skills
- Starts strong but gets thrown by resistance

Unacceptable

- Uses threats and coercion
- Received complaints about being heavy-handed
- Has been described as a bully
- Perceived as wanting "own way"
- Gives up much too easily

Phone Skills

Outstanding
- Effectively calms down angry callers
- Smooth under pressure
- Volume of calls handled consistently exceeds standards
- Handles high volume of calls with ease
- Advises staff on handling tough calls
- Callers call back and request him/her

Exceeds Expectations
- Has received compliments from clients
- Puts angry phone calls behind him/her
- Takes outstanding phone messages
- Transfers calls smoothly and accurately
- Sounds cheery even when busy

Meets Expectations
- Checks back with callers on hold every few minutes
- Answers all calls within four rings
- Returns calls within time promised
- Consistently meets call volume standard
- Keeps promises regarding returning calls
- Updates voice mail message at least daily

Needs Improvement
- Sometimes sounds rushed to customers
- Lacks understanding of phone equipment
- Frequently handles fewer calls than expected
- Leaves poor telephone messages for others
- Uncomfortable using voice mail
- Sometimes impatient or flustered

Unacceptable
- Customers often hang up due to wait

- Complaints received about phone manners
- Lost sales due to phone interactions
- Often does not return calls
- Hangs up abruptly
- Frequently becomes too informal with callers
- Many requests to speak to supervisor

Physical Abilities

Outstanding
- Seems never to become fatigued
- Performs all physical aspects of job flawlessly
- Exceedingly agile
- Makes sure actions are always performed safely
- Can lift ___ pounds above job requirement

Exceeds Expectations
- Rarely misses work due to illness
- Takes care of self
- Excellent depth perception
- Moves quickly without sacrificing safety
- Performs well even when under the weather

Meets Expectations
- Strong enough to meet job requirements
- Sufficient stamina to meet job requirements
- Can lift 40 pounds as per job requirement
- Moves safely around equipment
- Understands and respects own limitations

Needs Improvement
- Becomes uncoordinated under stress
- Lacks some fine motor skills
- Sometimes drops tools
- Bumps into things

Unacceptable
- Safety risk due to clumsiness
- Prone to injury on the job
- Physically unfit for job demands
- Dangerous to self and others
- Comes to work physically unready (e.g., hung over)

Planning and Scheduling

Outstanding
- Overcomes delays caused by others
- Copes well with problems beyond his/her control
- Helps others stay organized and on time
- Others regularly rely on his/her scheduling abilities
- Excellent contingency planner

Exceeds Expectations
- Does not overcommit self
- Has never created scheduling conflicts
- Plans practical and doable
- Anticipates where plans can go wrong

Meets Expectations
- Develops both long- and short-term plans
- Anticipates needs of project
- Using planning tools effectively
- Makes use of automated scheduling tools

Needs Improvement
- Can't see big picture in planning
- Doesn't consult others when required
- Avoids planning responsibilities
- Leaves planning until last minute

Unacceptable
- Cannot schedule for others
- Fails to plan for any contingencies
- Creates unworkable schedules
- Neglects to tell others of schedule changes

Political Skills

Outstanding
- Understands big picture
- Politically astute
- Uses power with discretion
- Exceptionally skilled at dealing with people at all levels of the organization
- Exceptionally skilled at choosing when to follow and when to lead

Exceeds Expectations
- Influences others without offending
- Accepts superiors' use of power
- Gets along well with people in different situations
- Seen as "peacemaker" by peers
- Can be trusted to handle politically sensitive situations
- Unintimidated by titles or others' power

Meets Expectations
- Compromises effectively
- Respects others' positions in organization
- Sensitive to office politics
- Seeks to minimize politics when possible
- Works well with subordinates
- Accepts prerogative of executive to decide issues

Needs Improvement
- Requires reining in
- Argues trivial points
- Seen as difficult by others
- Wields power unnecessarily
- Sometimes unaware of politically sensitive situations
- Often in conflict with peers

Unacceptable

- Often offends others
- Speaks without regard for others' reactions
- Argues for sake of argument
- Questions authority without valid reasons
- Doesn't work well with superiors
- Unaware of political implications of most situations

Potential for Advancement

Outstanding
- Effective leader without formal power
- Has stood in for supervisor without problems
- Eager for new challenges
- Has undertaken formal study for advancement
- Learns quickly and in depth
- Has potential to advance to high levels in the organization

Exceeds Expectations
- Quickly mastered current job
- Often helps solve others' problems
- Developed skills and abilities without prompting
- Pursues independent self-development

Meets Expectations
- Learns effectively over time
- Does current job acceptably
- Willing to go extra mile

Needs Improvement
- Learns slowly
- Repeats past solutions even when inappropriate
- Unaware of areas that need improvement
- Would require coaching in supervisory skills

Unacceptable
- Does not seem to have the capabilities to rise above current position
- Has not generated the confidence of others required for promotion
- Cannot see this employee in higher levels
- Cannot cope with complex decision making

Problem Solving

Outstanding

- Highly proficient and creative at solving problems
- Identifies problems in own area and develops resourceful solutions
- Weighs cost/benefit of many solutions to a problem
- Always addresses root causes in solutions
- Anticipates problems and solves before they develop
- Analyzes problems thoroughly and takes appropriate action

Exceeds Expectations

- Recognizes similarities among situations and appropriately addresses them
- Thorough in analyzing and developing solutions
- Knows when a problem warrants solving
- Always makes recommendations when a problem surfaces
- Develops alternative solutions to problems

Meets Expectations

- Satisfactory problem-solving skills
- Can analyze facts, information, and evidence logically
- Solutions to problems go beyond surface causes
- Recommends solutions to problems
- Sometimes will anticipate problems
- Uses good judgment and information in solving problems

Needs Improvement

- Generates solutions that don't always solve problems
- Knows solutions but doesn't recommend them
- Fails to identify underlying or systemic problems ➡

- Fails to completely analyze problems
- Doesn't recognize trends in recurring problems

Unacceptable

- Has insufficient problem-solving skills
- Weak problem-analysis skills
- Solutions address only surface problems
- Finds problems but doesn't solve them
- Doesn't generate solutions for problems
- Lets others find and fix problems

Productivity

Outstanding
- A star producer
- High productivity, high safety
- Produces more than anyone else in the department
- Wastes no time on small talk; she/he is all work
- Produced 3,432 units with a .03% reject rate
- Sold four units, surpassing goal by 50%
- Closed 98% of customer issues in first contact

Exceeds Expectations
- Above-average productivity
- Has helped others improve productivity
- Frequently above standards in production
- Maintains safety and quality
- Completed all four projects at a cost 12% below budget
- Installed three new systems on time with one callback

Meets Expectations
- Produces within standards
- Accurate and diligent producer
- Meets production goals while keeping quality high
- Handled 140 calls on average, per month
- Conducted five training days a month with reps in the Northeast region
- Does not sacrifice quality for quantity
- Tracks down problems that interfere with productivity

Needs Improvement
- Quantity is acceptable, but quality is low
- Distracted by trivial, unessential issues
- Speed is good, but accuracy is hurting overall rates

➡

- Needs to increase his/her productivity rates
- Missed production goals ____ times last year
- Generally produces well, but needs to maintain his/her machines better for fewer breakdowns

Unacceptable
- One of the lowest producers in the department
- Hasn't increased productivity despite coaching
- Work needs to be checked by others
- Production rate and quality are consistently low
- Productivity has been below standards for ____ of 12 months
- Average call length was 5.5 minutes, when the target is 2.0
- Her department responded to only 75% of customer inquiries within one day

Product Knowledge

Outstanding

- In-depth knowledge of all products
- Can explain product benefits to customers in ways that always address their problems
- Consistently recommends best product for customer
- Often praised by customers for expertise
- Makes it a point to keep up to date on competitors' products
- Knows all technical specifications of all our products
- Translates features to benefits for customer with confidence

Exceeds Expectations

- Partial knowledge of all or most products
- Customers request advice about products
- Has received positive comments from customers
- Makes suggestions to improve product line
- Familiar with competitors' products

Meets Expectations

- Familiar with product line
- Gives credible product descriptions to most customers
- Demonstrates proper use of product
- Effectively troubleshoots product problems

Needs Improvement

- Superficial knowledge of most products
- Often needs help explaining some products
- Customers sometimes ask to speak someone more expert
- Ineffective teacher on use of product
- Often relies on customer's expertise

Unacceptable

- Lacks critical product knowledge
- Presents incorrect product information to customers
- Loses sales as a result of lack of knowledge
- Almost never matches customer need with proper product

Professionalism

Outstanding

- Balances formality and friendliness
- Others ask for guidance
- Coaches other staff on professionalism
- Known by customers as honest and ethical
- Excellent spokesperson for company

Exceeds Expectations

- Almost never offends others
- Coworkers respect and listen to
- Regularly updates self on professional ethics
- Treats people equally despite their differences

Meets Expectations

- No valid complaints about conduct in last year
- Dresses according to function and expectations
- Rarely makes judgment errors in department
- Follows professional standards for job

Needs Improvement

- Sometimes cuts corners under pressure
- Tends to be difficult under pressure
- Has some gaps in understanding of professional conduct
- Rejects ideas of others in offhand way

Unacceptable

- Has made serious errors of judgment in past year
- Has offended several people during last year
- Does not follow through on commitments
- Sacrifices honesty for sales

Programming Skills

Outstanding
- Others can easily understand and alter code written
- Instructs and helps other programmers
- Has developed innovative ways to reduce computer load
- Solicits feedback on own work

Exceeds Expectations
- Creates excellently documented code
- Creates tight, efficient code
- Works well with minimum supervision
- Provides suggestions to analysts when needed
- Can work long hours when required to finish project

Meets Expectations
- Follows company procedures for coding
- Formats code well
- Debugs own code well before sending it on
- Competent in needed programming languages
- Follows system analyst's specification
- Clarifies specifications when needed

Needs Improvement
- Documentation sparse or difficult to understand
- Confused programming with system analysis
- Programs accurately but slowly
- Lacks depth of understanding of programming language
- Needs upgrading in program testing

Unacceptable
- Changes code without telling anyone

- Alters program specifications without consulting with client
- Code has many bugs
- Consistently misses deadlines
- Has caused project delays in past year
- Has difficulty working with [programming language]
- Has not improved in last two years

Project Management

Outstanding
- Understands the nuances of project planning
- Has complete mastery of Microsoft Project
- Brings projects in
- Knows how to select the best team to undertake a project
- Superior at coordinating resources needed to complete a project
- Communicates well with all project team members so problems don't occur
- Successfully dealt with five difficult problems that could have stalled project
- Interacts effectively with all stakeholders in project

Exceeds Expectations
- Makes effective use of Gantt and PERT charts
- Meets project budgets and timeframes
- Has communication system for keeping all project team members informed
- Accurately estimates project budgets
- Developed systems for keeping projects on track
- Effectively brings projects to closure

Meets Expectations
- Works well with project team members
- Effectively deals with problems when they arise
- Effectively uses project planning tools
- Projects usually come in no more than 5% over budget

Needs Improvement
- Does not fully understand project planning tools

➡

- Materials arrive at project either too early or too late
- Team members sometimes complain they are not fully informed
- Three projects came in ___% over budget
- Needs of external stakeholders not considered

Unacceptable
- Project timeframes frequently are not meant
- Steps in project poorly planned resulting in wasted resources and time
- Cannot understand how to use Microsoft Project
- Did not select the right people for the project team
- Two projects came in more than 25% over budget

Quality Management

Outstanding

- Conscious of customer requirements and makes sure defect-free products are always delivered
- Processes operate to deliver only 99.9% defect-free outputs
- Has all processes documented
- Conscientiously practices continuous improvement of processes
- Developed training course that resulted in all line personnel using SPC to improve processes
- Rework and scrap costs reduced by ___%

Exceeds Expectations

- Rarely loses focus on quality
- Continuous improvement a constant focus
- Consistently meets goals for costs and quality of outputs
- Uses SPC to measure and improve processes
- Shares information and resources to help others improve
- An effective advocate of SPC
- Had only a ___% defect rate
- Has delivered accurately and on time to 23 clients requesting samples

Meets Expectations

- Quality of outputs meets standards
- Practices quality control techniques
- Has mastered SPC techniques
- Understands how to analyze and improve processes
- Defect rates meet company standards

➡

- Understands how to analyze and improve processes
  Understands how to analyze and improve processe
- Takes customer needs into consideration in work
- Makes wise use of resources

Needs Improvement

- Does not have adequate understanding of SPC techniques
- Defect rate in some processes unacceptable
- XYZ project ___% over budget because of errors
- Scrap and rework costs exceeded budget by ___%
- On 3 occasions, colleague had to redo work
- Customers returned ___% of packages with parts missing

Unacceptable

- Defects greatly exceed standards
- Does not understand or practice SPC
- Makes errors frequently in his/her work
- Production runs averaged 70% acceptance rate
- Wastes resources
- Doesn't proof work or get it proofed before it goes to client

Quality of Work

Outstanding
- Work is consistently without error
- Takes special cautions to prevent errors
- Consistently receives praise for work quality
- Other employees use his/her work as model
- Customers regularly send commendations about work

Exceeds Expectations
- Leads group in reducing errors in work
- Has received commendations from five customers
- Work is regularly completed on time and error free
- Output quality makes it easy for others to do their jobs
- Focuses on continuously improving quality

Meets Expectations
- Work is regularly error free
- Quality of work meets standards
- Seeks training to learn how to improve quality
- Works well with customers to assure quality
- Makes use of quality improvement techniques
- Works well with other employees to ensure quality

Needs Improvement
- Employees complain about quality of his/her work
- Mistakes caused work stoppage on two occasions
- Does not pay enough attention to quality issues
- Needs to focus on reducing error rate
- Needs to apply training received to improve quality of outputs

Unacceptable
- On five occasions, errors caused work stoppage

- Defects in outputs caused one customer to choose another vendor
- Does not understand how to improve quality of outputs
- Quality is not a priority

Quantity of Work

Outstanding
- Overcomes obstacles to hitting targets
- Helps others achieve their targets
- Diagnoses barriers to producing desired quantities
- Fixes problems and barriers to hitting targets
- In top 5% in sales each month

Exceeds Expectations
- Exceeded target by __% last year
- Effective at dealing with obstacles
- Suggested ways for everyone to increase quantity of output
- Contributes to profit margin

Meets Expectations
- Ordinarily achieves targets
- Produces well without slowing others down
- Takes on challenge of difficult quotas
- Produces __ items per month

Needs Improvement
- 10% below target last two years
- Lacks a few skills needed to increase production
- Hasn't volunteered for skill upgrades
- Output sometimes affected when under stress

Unacceptable
- Interferes with coworkers' production
- Unwilling to learn how to improve
- Seriously below targets for one year
- Doesn't show concern for missing targets

Research Abilities

Outstanding
- Zeros in on essential information
- Consistently prepared with information before needed
- Excellent at reconciling conflicting information
- Accurately interprets complex statistical data

Exceeds Expectations
- Finds needed information quickly
- Evaluates contradictory information
- Determines relative importance of information
- Ferrets out difficult-to-find information

Meets Expectations
- Completes assigned research projects
- Prepares research reports on time
- Understands technical research papers in own field
- Sets realistic deadlines for gathering information

Needs Improvement
- Doesn't use all research tools available
- Sometimes suffers information overload
- Reports research findings in confusing way
- Cannot research outside of specialized field

Unacceptable
- Mistakes trivial information for important
- Does not distinguish between wheat and chaff
- Conclusions often muddy the waters
- Consistently misinterprets data

Resource Use

Outstanding
- Creates excellent return on investment
- Excellent resource forecaster
- Has introduced cost-saving measures
- Uses innovative ways to save

Exceeds Expectations
- Works within budget and allocated personnel
- Required more resources only due to emergency
- Suggests ways to save money and resources
- Considers various ways to complete job at less cost

Meets Expectations
- Coordinates resource use with others
- Rarely needs overtime to get job done
- Returns resources so others can use
- Treats resources carefully

Needs Improvement
- Takes resources without informing others
- Uses resources designated for others
- Consistently underanticipates resources needed
- Sometimes forgets others may need same resources

Unacceptable
- Rarely comes in on budget
- Negatively impacts others' work
- Received complaints about hoarding resources
- Has damaged resources needed by others

Safety

Outstanding
- Always adheres to safety rules and procedures
- Consistently safe
- Has had no safety infractions
- Wears appropriate safety gear on shop floor at all times
- Tolerates no safety violations
- Monitors employees' safety practices at least one hour every day
- Always reminds staff of safety issues in morning meeting

Exceeds Expectations
- Has excellent safety record
- Encourages safe practices often
- Very safety conscious
- Team had only one minor accident in hazardous work
- Enforces safety very strictly

Meets Expectations
- Performs all work within safety guidelines
- Had good safety record
- A safe worker
- Values safe working procedures
- Maintains vehicle strictly according to maintenance manual

Needs Improvement
- Uses safety equipment only when told
- Failed to wear safety goggles twice in last quarter
- Missed work three times owing to unsafe practices
- Does not enforce safety practices among employees
- Fails to adhere to safe work practices

- Sacrifices safety for productivity

Unacceptable

- Has violated safety guidelines many times
- Failed to adhere to safety rules ___ times in one month
- Ignores safety rules
- Tolerates unsafe or hazardous conditions
- Repeatedly ignores "no smoking" signs
- Frequently does not wear safety equipment

Sales Ability

Outstanding

- Is among our finest sales representatives
- Has closed all our large sales
- A role model for other sales people
- Always makes the sales target
- Closed 33% of sales where employee was called in as a product specialist
- Exceeded sales target by 23%
- Successfully leveraged our success with company X to have it try our latest version of product Z
- Powerful openings and closings
- Clearly understands clients' needs

Exceeds Expectations

- Maintains excellent relations with clients
- Very good openings
- Always closes with some action for prospect to take
- Represents our company very well
- Comes across as an educator more than a sales representative—and this works well!
- Introduced product X to three new markets—auto, computer, and appliance
- Employee's clients referred three other companies to us, citing the individual's good service
- Great closer!
- Sends birthday, anniversary, holiday cards to clients and their staff

Meets Expectations

- A dedicated salesperson
- Consistently makes sales quota

- Rarely misses sales quota
- Could become a very good salesperson soon
- Persuades more often than not
- Stocks car with appropriate samples on a weekly basis for all upcoming calls
- Successfully had our product specifications included in prospect X's RFP
- Maintains folders with newspaper articles and clippings for each account and delivers them on the sales call
- Good product knowledge, but weak on closing

Needs Improvement
- Is almost making his/her quota
- Needs to learn a lot more about our products
- Needs to learn more about sales techniques
- Is uncomfortable presenting to large client groups
- Maintains good relations with prospects, but doesn't close

Unacceptable
- Met only 80% of quota
- Knows few sales techniques
- Has weak relationships with clients
- Sales ability is very poor
- Needs to improve sales in area of responsibility immediately

Stress, Ability to Work Under

Outstanding

- Shows an outstanding ability to manage her/his own stress
- Demonstrates calm when most others are panicking
- Never raises his/her voice no matter what the circumstances
- Is relaxed and calm in the face of major problems
- Always responds to provocation with calm and grace
- Always helps others deal with stress

Exceeds Expectations

- Does a very good job of managing stress from the job
- Is mostly calm in stressful situations
- Frequently helps others deal with stress
- Rarely raises his/her voice in stressful situations

Meets Expectations

- Manages the stress from the job satisfactorily
- Generally shows calm when faced with stressful situations
- Occasionally helps others manage the stress from the job
- Will raise his/her voice occasionally in stressful situations

Needs Improvement

- Must improve his/her ability to manage stress
- Often can't manage the stress from his job
- Often raises his/her voice in stressful situations
- Gets nervous and avoids making decisions in stressful situations
- Rarely helps others deal with a stressful situation

Unacceptable

- Is frequently nervous and on edge
- Never handles project changes with calmly
- Frequently yells and screams in stressful situations
- Rarely is relaxed and speaks quietly
- Spreads increased stress to others
- Hardly ever manages his/her stress
- Is insensitive to others' stress
- Never helps others deal with stressful situations

Supervisory Skills

Outstanding
- Exceptionally dedicated and sensitive to employee needs
- Actions have resulted in strong staff loyalty
- Excellent mentor to employees
- Provides excellent and regular feedback to employees
- Has mastery of all staff jobs
- Excellent team leader
- Successfully removes obstacles that get in staff's way
- Has the affection and support of staff

Exceeds Expectations
- Supervises staff with skill
- Excellent staff motivator
- Lays out projects clearly for staff
- Assigns job responsibilities to stretch staff
- Provides opportunities for staff to develop
- Understands workflow and technologies used

Meets Expectations
- Appropriately trains staff
- Explains new projects clearly to reduce errors
- Delegates when appropriate
- Keeps management informed
- Acknowledges and rewards good performances
- Sets goals with staff

Needs Improvement
- Occasionally heavy-handed
- Overdelegates
- Poor planning results in staff overload
- Tends to restrict learning opportunities
- Could listen more to staff

➡

Unacceptable

- Frequently critical of staff
- Avoids communicting with staff
- Staff shows little respect for person or position
- Hoards information
- Has had more than one legitimate grievance filed
- Does not respect confidentiality issues
- Always uses command-and-control approach

Teamwork

Outstanding
- Shows exceptional teamwork
- Drives others to exceed goals
- Works within and between teams knowledgeably and capably
- Manages the team process with great skill
- Serves as the head of _____ teams

Exceeds Expectations
- Gets along well with fellow team members
- Works well on teams
- Performs team-assigned work on time and effectively
- Keeps others informed of status of projects affecting them, when responsible for doing so
- Creates strong teams

Meets Expectations
- Serves as an effective team member
- Communicates well with other teams
- Mostly an optimistic team player
- Dedicated to team goals
- Heads _____ teams and serves on _____ teams

Needs Improvement
- Motivated more for his/her own goals than those of team
- Not seen as a team player
- Has worked against team goals on occasion
- Fails to coordinate work of his/her teams
- Was reassigned from the Safety team earlier this year

Unacceptable
- Does not work on teams well

- Has consistently failed to achieve goals as team member
- Doesn't contribute to team mission
- Does not communicate project status to affected groups when responsible for doing so
- Has been taken off _____ teams

Technical Skills

Outstanding
- Understands all work procedures and methods
- Shows technical excellence in all areas of her/his position
- Adapts well to technological developments relevant in his/her area
- Shows outstanding technical skills
- Has learned new tools to teach to others
- Uses own time to update skills
- Maintains all certifications
- Anticipates and acquires skills before they are needed
- Creates or fixes job tools as necessary

Exceeds Expectations
- Able to learn new job-relevant skills when needed
- Demonstrates both skill and understanding of job tools
- Seen as expert helper by peers
- Takes leadership role in acquiring new technology

Meets Expectations
- Mastered skills needed for job
- Operates job machinery effectively
- Has trouble dealing with computerized machinery
- Able to acquire and use new skills as job requires
- Consistently follows safety and security procedures

Needs Improvement
- Retraining needed in one or two skills
- Does not have skills in problem prevention
- New technology has outstripped existing understanding
- Lack of use has eroded a few skills

➡

Unacceptable

- Understands very few work procedures or methods
- Demonstrates few technical skills
- Needs improvement in level of knowledge in many areas
- Has allowed certifications to lapse
- Does not alter methods to keep current with technological changes
- Lacks majority of skills needed
- Hasn't benefited from technical skill training
- Unaware of lack of crucial skills

Time Management Skills

Outstanding
- Rarely any wasted effort or time
- Paces self to avoid burnout
- Makes effective use of time management tools
- Excellent at prioritizing of tasks
- Able to deal with emergencies

Exceeds Expectations
- Never procrastinates
- Creates atmosphere for good concentration
- Works to tight deadlines
- Delegates when appropriate

Meets Expectations
- Prioritizes effectively
- Usually meets deadlines
- Does not promise what can't be delivered in specific timeframe
- Manages interruptions well
- Effectively uses time management tools (e.g., planners, computers)
- Does not overextend self
- Accurately estimates how long work takes
- Outlines tasks with timeline to finish overall assignment
- Breaks down task or project into workable parts

Needs Improvement
- Occasionally procrastinates
- Allows people and events to interrupt when not necessary
- Needs to use a daily planner
- Tries to do everything herself/himself ➡

- Is easily distracted from task on hand
- Does not deal well with time crises
- Loses track of what the job involves

Unacceptable
- Often does not meet deadlines
- Easily distracted
- Does not understand how to use time management tools
- Does not prioritize tasks
- Unable to distinguish important from trivial activities
- Spends too much time socializing

Appendix A

Ten Mistakes Managers Make When Conducting Performance Appraisals

Robert Bacal

Performance appraisals aren't fun. But a lot of the time they are agonizing because many managers have some misconceptions about the process and why they do it, and the mistakes they make in light of this end up destroying a process that is important to everyone (or should be).

Mistake #1: Spending more time on performance appraisal than performance *planning* or ongoing performance communication. Performance appraisal is the end of a process that goes on all the time—a process that is based on good communication between manager and employee. So, more time should be spent preventing performance problems than evaluating at the end of the year. When managers do good things during the year, the appraisal is easy to do and comfortable, because there won't be any surprises.

Mistake #2: Comparing employees with each other. Want to create bad feelings, damage morale, get staff to compete so badly they will not work as a team? Then rank staff or compare staff. A guaranteed technique. And heck, not only can a manager create friction among staff, but the manager can become a great target for that hostility too. A bonus!

Mistake #3: Forgetting appraisal is about improvement, not blame. We do appraisal to improve performance, not find a donkey to pin a tail on or blame. Managers who forget this end up developing staff who don't trust them, or even can't stand them. That's because the blaming process is pointless and doesn't help anyone. If there is to be a point to performance appraisal, it should be getting manager and employee working together to have everyone get better.

Mistake #4: Thinking a rating form is an objective, impartial tool. Many companies use rating forms to evaluate employees (you know, the 1-5 ratings?). They do that because it's faster than doing it right. The problem comes when managers believe that those ratings are in some way "real," or anything but subjective, often vague judgments that are bound to be subjective and inaccurate. By the way, if you have two people rate the same employee, the chances of them agreeing are very small. *That's* subjective. Say it to yourself over and over. Ratings are subjective. Rating forms are subjective. Rating forms are not behavioral.

Mitake #5: Stopping performance appraisal when a person's salary is no longer tied to the appraisals. Lots of managers do this. They conduct appraisals so long as they have to do so to justify or withhold a pay increase. When staff hit their salary ceiling, or pay is not connected to appraisal and performance, managers don't bother. Dumb. Performance appraisal is *for* improving performance. It isn't just about pay (although some think it is *only* about pay). If nothing else, everyone needs feedback on their jobs, whether there is money involved or not.

Mistake #6: Believing they are in a position to accurately assess staff. Managers delude themselves into believing they can assess staff performance, even if they hardly ever see their staff actually doing their jobs, or the results of their jobs. Not possible. Most managers aren't in a position to monitor staff consistently enough to be able to assess well. And, besides what manager wants to do that or has the time? And, what employee wants their manager perched, watching their every mood? That's why appraisal is a partnership between employee and manager.

Mistake #7: Cancelling or postponing appraisal meetings. Happens a whole lot. I guess because nobody likes to do them, so managers will postpone them at the drop of a hat. Why is this bad? It says to employees that the process is unimportant or phony. If managers aren't willing to commit to the process, then they shouldn't do it at all. Employees are too smart not to notice the low priority placed on appraisals.

Mistake #8: Measuring or appraising the trivial. Fact of life: The easiest things to measure or evaluate are the least important things with respect to doing a job. Managers are quick to define customer service as "answering the phone within three rings" or some such thing. That's easy to measure if you want to. What's *not* easy to measure is the overall quality of service that will get and keep customers. Measuring overall customer service is hard, so many managers don't do it. But they will measure the trivial.

Mistake #9: Surprising employees during appraisal. Want to really waste your time and create bad performance? This is a guaranteed technique. Don't talk to staff during the year. When they mess up, don't deal with it at the time but *save* it up. Then, at the appraisal meeting, truck out everything saved up in the bank and dump it in the employee's lap. That'll show 'em who is boss!

Mistake #10: Thinking all employees and all jobs should be assessed in exactly the same way using the same procedures. Do all employees need the same things to improve their performance? Of course not. Some need specific feedback. Some don't. Some need more communication than others. And of course jobs are all different Do you think we can evaluate the CEO of Ford using the same approach as we use for the person who cleans the factory floor? Of course not. So, why do managers insist on evaluating the receptionist using the same tools and criteria as the civil engineers in the office? It's not smart. One size does not fit all. Actually why do managers do this? Mostly because the personnel or human resource office leans on them to do so. It's almost understandable, but that doesn't make it any less excusable.

This article is based on the books *Performance Management: Why Doesn't It Work?* and *Performance Management,* a title in the Briefcase Books series published by McGraw-Hill. Copyright © 1999 by Robert Bacal. This article may not be reproduced without permission.

Appendix B

Seven Mistakes Employees Make During Performance Appraisals

Robert Bacal

Generally, when performance appraisal goes awry, the primary cause has little to do with employees. For the most part, employees take their cues from management and human resources. However, when individual employees perceive the process in negative ways, they can damage even the best of appraisal processes.

Mistake #1: Focusing on the appraisal forms. Performance appraisal isn't about the forms (although, often managers and HR treat it as such). The ultimate purpose of performance appraisal is to allow employees and managers to improve continuously and to remove barriers to job success. In other words, to make everyone better. Forms don't make people better, and are simply a way of recording basic information for later reference. If the focus is getting the forms "done," without thought and effort, the whole process becomes at best a waste of time, and at worst, insulting.

Mistake #2: Not preparing beforehand. Preparing for performance appraisal helps the employee focus on the key issue—performance improvement—and examine his or her performance in a more objective way (see "Defensiveness" below). Unfortunately, many employees walk into the appraisal meeting not having thought about the review period, and so are unprepared to present their points of view. Being unprepared means being a reactive participant, or being a passive participant. Neither are going to help manager or employee. Employees can prepare by reviewing their work beforehand, identifying any barriers they faced in doing their jobs, and refamiliarizing themselves with their job descriptions, job responsibilities, and any job performance expectations set with the manager.

Mistake #3: Defensiveness. We tend to take our jobs seriously and personally, making it more difficult to hear others' comments about our work, particularly when they are critical. Even constructive criticism is often hard to hear. If employees enter into the discussion with an attitude of "defending," then it's almost impossible to create the dialogue necessary for performance improvement. That doesn't mean employees can't present their own opinions and perceptions, but it does mean that they should be presented in a calm, factual manner, rather than a defensive, emotional way. Of course, if managers are inept in the appraisal process, it makes it very difficult to avoid this defensiveness.

Mistake #4: Not communicating during the year. Employees need to know how they are doing all year round, not just at appraisal time. Generally it is primarily management's responsibility to ensure that there are no surprises at appraisal time. Often managers discuss both positives and negatives of employee performance throughout the year, but this is unfortunately not a universal practice. It's in the employees interests to open up discussion about performance during the year, even if the manager does not initiate it. The sooner employees know where they are at, and what they need to change (or keep doing), the sooner problems can be fixed. In fact many problems can be prevented if they are caught early enough. Even if managers aren't creating that communication, employees can and should. It's a shared responsibility.

Mistake #5: Not clarifying enough. Life would be much easier if managers were perfect, but they aren't. Some communicate and explain well. Some don't. Some are aggravating and some not. At times employees won't be clear about their manager's reasoning or comments, or what a manager is suggesting. That could be because the manager isn't clear himself/herself, or simply isn't good at explaining. However, unless employees clarify when they aren't sure about the reasoning or explanations, they won't know what they need to do to improve their future job performance. It's important to leave the appraisal meeting having a good understanding of what's been said. If that's not possible, clarification can occur after the meeting, or down the road, if that's more appropriate.

Mistake #6: Allowing one-sidedness. Performance appraisals work best when both participants are active and expressing their positions and ideas. Some employees are uncomfortable doing that, and while managers should be creating a climate where employees are comfortable, some managers aren't good at it. Performance appraisal time is an excellent time for employees to make suggestions about things that could be changed to improve performance, about how to remove barriers to job success, and about ways to increase productivity. Remember also that managers can't read minds. The better managers will work with employees to help them do their jobs more effectively, but they can't know how they can help unless employees provide them with good, factual information or, even better, concrete ideas.

Mistake #7: Focusing on appraisal as a way of getting more money. Unfortunately, many organizations tie employee pay to appraisal results, which puts employee and manager on opposite sides. Employees in such systems tend to focus too much on the money component, although that focus is certainly understandable. It's also understandable when employees in such systems become hesitant to reveal shortcomings or mistakes. But it's still dumb. If employees' main purpose is to squeeze as much of an increase out of the company, and the managers try to keep increases as small as possible, it becomes totally impossible to focus on what ultimately matters over the long term, which is continuous performance improvement and success for everyone.

Pay *is* important, but it is not the only issue related to the appraisal focus. If employees enter into the process willing to defend their own positions in factual and fair ways and to work with managers, the process can become much more pleasant. If not, it can become a war.

Conclusion

The major responsibilities for setting performance appraisal tone and climate rest with managers and the human resources department. However, even when managers and human resources do their jobs well, employees who come at the process with a negative or defensive approach are not likely to gain from the process or to prosper over the long term. The constant key is for employees to participate actively and assertively, but to keep a problem-solving mindset and keep focused on how things can be improved in the future. No matter who initiates it, performance appraisal is about positive open communication between employee and manager.

About the Authors

Douglas Max is Managing Director, LR Communication Systems, Berkeley Heights, NJ. He is responsible for all marketing and sales, selection, training, and supervision of staff of 15. His firm designs and conduct on-site seminars in writing and presentation skills. He is also moderator of TRDEV, the largest training-oriented e-mail discussion group on the Web. He has an MA in Industrial/Organizational Psychology from the University of Missouri at St. Louis. Visit his Web site at www.lrcom.com.

Robert Bacal is an accomplished consultant, book author, trainer, and public speaker. He is the author of *The Complete Idiot's Guide to Dealing with Difficult Employees* and *The Complete Idiot's Guide to Consulting* (Alpha Books) and *Performance Management*, a title in the Briefcase Books series (McGraw-Hill). Under the imprint of Bacal & Associates, Bacal has also published the *Defusing Hostile Customers Workbook* and *Conflict Prevention in the Workplace*. Visit his popular Web site at www.work911.com.

PERFECT PHRASES
for...

MANAGERS

Perfect Phrases for Managers and Supervisors

Perfect Phrases for Setting Performance Goals

Perfect Phrases for Performance Reviews

Perfect Phrases for Motivating and Rewarding Employees

Perfect Phrases for Documenting Employee Performance Problems

Perfect Phrases for Business Proposals and Business Plans

Perfect Phrases for Customer Service

Perfect Phrases for Executive Presentations

Perfect Phrases for Business Letters

Perfect Phrases for the Sales Call

Perfect Phrases for Perfect Hiring

Perfect Phrases for Building Strong Teams

Perfect Phrases for Dealing with Difficult People

YOUR CAREER

Perfect Phrases for the Perfect Interview

Perfect Phrases for Resumes

Perfect Phrases for Negotiating Salary & Job Offers

Perfect Phrases for Cover Letters

Learn more.  Do more.

Visit mhprofessional.com/perfectphrases for a complete product listing.